the taste of a place

andalucía

Text © Chakula Press Ltd

All rights reserved. No part of this book
may be reproduced in any form without
written permission from the publisher.

Set in Gill Sans 8.5/11pt

Design by Price Watkins

A catalogue record for this book is available
from the British Library

ISBN 0-9542692-2-5

contents

Granada

Introduction

Inside, you will find:

The different and diverse eating experiences to be had around Andalucía – from simple tapas bars, and places serving traditional local cooking, to full-scale restaurants where you can sample the very best of Andalucian cuisine.

Details of the finest foods to buy in Andalucía, and where to buy them – from good basic local produce, to the region's top gourmet delicacies.

An introduction to Andalucía's wines – and not just sherry, which I'm a huge fan of, but also some fabulous reds and whites from the region's up-and-coming bodegas.

A selection of easy-to-do Andaluz recipes – to try at home or on holiday.

If your idea of Andalucía is based on a holiday break spent at the Costa del Sol, then you may not have had time to appreciate the uniquely important part that eating and drinking plays in the culture and society of the region. It's not always obvious but Andalucian cooking is at the very roots of European cuisine.

This book sets out to highlight the places in Andalucía – its restaurants, tapas bars, bodegas and shops – that I think are really worth investigating if you want to get a taste of this colourful region of culinary contrasts. And the recipe section offers you the chance to recreate this authentic taste in your own kitchen.

I think that the best way to discover somewhere new is to have a friend with you, one who's already in the know about the place you're visiting. And this book aims to be that friend. To help me to give you a true taste of Andalucía, I enlisted the aid and experience of Héloïse, Roger and Phil, whose opinions I value. We haven't tried to tell you everything. Like any friends, we have our own prejudices and idiosyncrasies – so you may not agree with absolutely everything we recommend, but we are impartial: no business has ever bought our favour, or paid to be mentioned in this book. And your views matter, too. If you think we've missed something or somewhere marvellous, then please do log on to the website www.thetasteofaplace.com and let us – and other readers – know about it.

Andalucian cuisine

Down on the sunny *costas*, with their staggering array of commercial eateries serving food from all over the world, it's difficult to get a clear idea of what Andalucian cuisine is all about. Indeed, it's hard enough sometimes to get an idea of what Andalucía is all about.

Gastronomic geography

For Andalucía is not just the *costas*, any more than Portugal is just the Algarve. The region is more or less the size of Portugal, in fact. Look at the map, and you'll find it's a massive slab of Spain, some 90,000 square kilometres in area, with mountains, rivers, valleys, plains, hills, marshes and deserts, as well as those 700 kilometres of coastline, and a southernmost tip almost within touching distance of Africa. In hard geographical terms, this is a region that's big enough and varied enough to have at least four quite different micro-climates – including the arid badlands in the east, the damp freshwater marshes in the west, the sun-drenched coastal resorts down at sea level, and the magnificent Sierra Nevada towering over two miles high. In the Cabo de Gata and the Sierra de Grazalema respectively, Andalucía has both the driest and the wettest places in Spain. Such a great diversity has inevitably led to colourful contrasts in local culture, along with delicious variations in food and drink.

But what this means, above all, is that pinning down what makes a recipe Andalucian isn't always easy. In the Basque region of northern Spain, for example, there's a dish called *ajoarriero* (Ernest Hemingway's favourite, as it happens), which is made with cod, peppers and garlic. This is a basic recipe that is recognisable in homes and restaurants throughout the Basque area. No matter how a chef may decide to tweak it, to embellish it with his or her own personal signature, it nevertheless remains, quite clearly and unmistakably, *ajoarriero*.

Infinite variations

Not so in Andalucía. Here, there is no set recipe for anything. Until the current fashion for building bigger and better motorways across the valleys, this was a region where a visit to a neighbouring *pueblo* was likely to be a major exercise, with another mountain range forever coming into view. Consequently, housewives just went on cooking their food in their own individual way, without too many outside influences or interferences; with the result that *cocido andaluz*, Andalucian stew, which you'd imagine would be pretty much a standard dish of the region, does not conform to any single definitive recipe. Indeed, just to confuse matters, in many places this "national" dish goes by an entirely different name, *puchero*. You'll find a recipe for one version of it, by the way, on page 128.

Gazpacho is another example. It's probably Andalucía's most famous dish, but it doesn't take long to realise that the name actually refers to a whole family of soups – all with the same basic ingredients (garlic, bread, vinegar and oil), but with lots of possible additions. Tomato, onion and cucumber are the most common, but, depending where

you are in the region, the soup could also include almonds, broad beans, cumin, pine nuts, dried peppers, asparagus and even cherries. Not all at once, mind you! Our version, with almonds, and without cherries, is on page 115.

The variation is not just in how the food is cooked, either. It's also a matter of what the food consists of in the first place. The wetlands at the mouth of the Guadalquivir river are ideal for growing rice; the cold dry air of the sierras provides perfect conditions for curing hams; the coastlines, naturally, support an abundance of fish and seafood; while the market gardens – particularly in Almería, Huelva and on the "tropical" coast of Granada – grow a great range of fruit and vegetables. And in spite of the blossoming infrastructure, it's the nature of the local produce that still has the strongest influence on local recipes.

Out of Africa

On a larger scale, geography has played a powerful role in Andalucía's development too. With Spain being separated from the rest of Europe by the Pyrenees, and the region itself being divided from the rest of Spain by the Sierra Morena, Andalucía has seen most of its visitors – welcome and unwelcome – arriving from the south by sea. Phoenicians, Greeks, Carthaginians, Romans, Vandals and Visigoths had all put in an appearance before the Moors arrived in the eighth and ninth centuries. It was the Phoenicians who established Cádiz, for example; the Romans, for their part, planted olives and wheat for export back to Rome (along with certain local delicacies they'd discovered, such as saltfish and *garum* pickle). More importantly, though, they introduced wine – and this part of the world has been an important wine producer ever since. Sherry and Málaga wines were at one time the most sought-after wines

in the world, and despite the vagaries of fortune created by phylloxera, mass tourism and changing tastes, Andalucía remains one of the most exciting wine areas in Europe, with plenty of interesting fortified and table wines just waiting to be discovered – and rediscovered.

But even with this great wine heritage, by far the most important influence on Andalucía's cultural and culinary history has always been its proximity to North Africa. Along with the teachings of Mohammed, Arabic influences on art and architecture, and a new name for the country, Al-Andalus, the Moors brought with them a radically different agriculture, and the cultivation of new fruits and vegetables, including spinach and aubergines, broad beans, mint, quince and pomegranate; exotic spices too, such as cinnamon, nutmeg and saffron. They developed revolutionary irrigation systems, some of which are still

watering the fields today; and their influence on Spanish and European cuisine has been profound. It is from the Arabs who invaded Andalucía that the Western world acquired its basic dining convention of a set order of courses, ending up with sweet foods.

1492 and all that

It was to be another seven or eight hundred years before the cooking of southern Spain would see a similar revolution. At the end of the fifteenth century there was an important new invasion; but this time it was Spain's own conquest of the Americas. And once more Andalucía found itself at the cutting edge of European cuisine, as strange transatlantic ingredients began to arrive at the region's ports. It's hard now to imagine our foodstores without the produce that was first unloaded in those days on the docksides of Seville (yes, Seville) and Cádiz: tomatoes, potatoes, sweetcorns, pumpkins, sweet potatoes, peppers, green beans ... oh, yes, and chocolate.

This was a busy time for Spain. While she was conquering the Americas, she was also expelling Arabs and Jews in large numbers from all over the land – and Andalucía, the old *Al-Andalus* heartland of the Moors, was eventually purged, leaving the region to be gradually repopulated from elsewhere. You can sometimes spot traces of these great movements, in the way that dishes seem somehow to have acquired a number of different names: in and around Andalucía, for example, you'll find that the equivalent of ratatouille is variously called *pisto*, or *fritada*, or, sometimes, *alboronia*, which itself is derived from the Arabic *al-burunayah*.

Holy orders

It's a grim thought, but, at the time of these purges, you were far less likely to be expelled (or worse) as a Jew or a Moslem if you were openly eating pork. Indeed, the eating of pork has long had a profound influence in Spain, and it's generally been associated with Christianity. The Christian parts of Spain that remained unconquered by the Moors tended to be the northern regions that were too cold for olive trees, where consequently pigs were reared for their lard as well as their meat. The cool drying winds through the sierras produce some of the very best air-dried ham in the world, and pork is today a major feature of *Andaluz* gastronomy (see page 63).

In fact, the Christian monasteries and convents have generally been incubators of the old culinary traditions. Monks distilled anise liqueurs, helped to popularise the potato and tomato and, most famously, took over the Arab sweet-making traditions after the reconquest; biscuits and pastries are

Baeza

another key feature in the Andalucian gastronomic landscape (see page 48).

Naturally, food plays an important role in the festivities of the Christian church here. Take, for example, the carnival in Cádiz, one of the most important in Spain. It starts a month before Ash Wednesday, and one of the first great events is the *pestiñada*, when large quantities of *pestiños*, or honey pastries, are eaten in Plaza de San Francisco. The following week the *erizada* is celebrated in Plaza de la Viña, and the *ostionada* in Plaza de San Antonio: at the *erizada*, everyone eats *erizos de mar* (sea urchins); at the *ostionada*, it's masses of *ostiones* (Portuguese oysters) that are devoured. And all this festive eating isn't confined to Cádiz. Every town and village in Andalucía will have some sort of fiesta in honour of its own local produce – from a little village such as Riogordo, in the sierras behind Málaga, which celebrates its snails in May, to the great wine festival of Jerez in September. In fact, just about every week of the year, you'll find someone, somewhere, celebrating something edible.

The daily grind

Making use of what can be foraged from the countryside is always something to be thankful for, and always something to be celebrated. But in hard times, it's a matter of sheer necessity. Poverty has often been the mother of culinary invention in Andalucía, which has seen more than its share of hard times over the centuries. In the twentieth century, large parts of the population verged on starvation after the civil war. Travelling salesmen would even come round the villages with ham bones for rent. And a local dish of breadcrumbs fried in olive oil, *migas*, reminds us of how important it always was not to let stale bread go to waste.

It's hard to believe sometimes when you're surrounded by chic shops and wall-to-wall sunshine, but life is by no means always easy here. Even now, despite its huge tourist industry, Andalucía still has pockets where there is high unemployment. Among other Spaniards, the Andalucians are often jokingly regarded as lazy, but, as one local waiter explained: "We're not lazy. We're just good at looking after ourselves – and we've needed to be. In the past, when the government in Madrid just forgot all about us, the *campo* was our main source of food. And there are still people here who go out there in the mornings and come back with everything they need to eat."

Fried fish

With its rich diversity and its unique importance in the European culinary tradition, you might imagine that Andalucian cooking would enjoy a better reputation than it does. But ask another Spaniard what Andalucian food is like, and the reply is almost always the same: "fried fish" – *pescaito frito* – in a tone which implies you'll be lucky if it's any good, and there'll be nothing else to eat, either.

But below the surface, this simply isn't true: Andalucía is still the spiritual heartland of Spain – still *Al-Andalus*, with its horses and its *flamenco*. And it is still indubitably the origin of *tapas*, and the birthplace of *gazpacho*, and the home of sherry wines.

So, if the Andalucians are not over-reverential about their food (and who else would have a soup that translates as "son of a bitch"?) then perhaps that is because the enjoyment of life is still firmly at the top of their list of priorities. And their food, even with all its rich and colourful diversity, is just one of very many features that go to ensure that it stays there.

Eating out

All the best places

Andalucía, like most of the rest of Spain, eats late. It's a habit that is easy enough for a visiting foodie to slip into – as long as you remember to adopt the correct Andalucian eating routines. Concentrate now. Start by having a big breakfast.

The big breakfast

"He's just gone out for breakfast" is a refrain you will frequently encounter, mid-morning, when trying to contact somebody at work. "Try again in about an hour".

Breakfast, *el desayuno*, is taken seriously in Andalucía. People may do no more than gulp down a quick coffee at home before leaving for work, but most will want to pop out of the office later in the morning for further sustenance.

Alas, the dreaded Euro-regulations are creeping in, and the big breakfast is currently under siege. Notices are even beginning to appear in offices, warning that "breakfast is no longer a valid reason for being away from one's desk".

Still, no matter whose time it's being eaten in, breakfast in Andalucía generally involves something pretty substantial: large pieces of crusty or toasted bread, for instance, drizzled with olive oil, or spread with *zurrapa* and *chicharrones*, which are pork specialities in spiced lard. Tomato is also a popular accompaniment with bread or toast. You either rub half a tomato into the bread, Catalan-style, or you spoon on some freshly chopped tomato salsa (easy to make – you just whiz a tomato, a pinch of salt and sugar and two tablespoons of olive oil in a blender). Buns and rolls, toasted or oven-warmed, are typical too, as are pastries: the *mollete* is a soft roll usually eaten with oil; *bollo suizo* is a sugar-glazed bun eaten dripping with margarine or butter.

Chocolate y churros, a cup of thick chocolate served with pieces of deep-fried dough to dip in, is still a hugely popular mid-morning snack in Andalucía, especially among women who have finished their shopping and are meeting up with friends for a good gossip – even in the height of summer. It is also sometimes eaten before going to bed, as a sort of pre-dawn breakfast, after a long dance-till-you-drop night out on the tiles.

Coffee with milk (*café con leche*) is an essential. Traditionally the drink is served in a glass, but tourists are often given theirs in a cup. According to one waiter who busily serves thousands of breakfasts on the Plaza Bib-Rambla in Granada: "coffee tastes much better when drunk from a glass, and chocolate is better from a cup." Insist, therefore, on your coffee *en un vaso*.

Coffee comes in various strengths. The Café Central in Málaga has decorative tiles on the wall depicting nine types of coffee (all in a glass, of course), from the no-milk *café solo*, to a *nube* (cloud) which has a tiny amount of black coffee in the bottom of a glass made up with milk. Other popular options are *solo cortado* or *solo corto*, a small coffee with a dash of milk; *descafeinado*, a decaffeinated coffee; *café con hielo*, served with a glass of ice, and wonderful in a heatwave; and an old favourite, *carajillo*, which is a café solo with a dash of brandy in it.

A late lunch

Lunch, *el almuerzo* or *la comida*, is the main meal of the day for most Spaniards, and suitably fortified as you are with chocolate and churros, you certainly won't feel like eating until at least 2pm, which is the start of the Spanish lunch hour. Well, lunch two or three hours, actually. Some restaurants may open as early as one o'clock, but usually only to serve tourists. Two-thirty is the busy time, when you will have most difficulty in getting a table; by about three-thirty things will have eased off a bit and you may well be the only non-Spaniard there. Most places serve lunch until about four.

The *menú del día* is a fixed-price menu offering three courses, with bread and a drink. In bars and restaurants geared to Spanish workers the *menú* will be basic but good value – and this is when dishes that are generally considered unhealthy to eat at other times of the day make an appearance: dishes like *paella* or *migas* (fried breadcrumbs). These are thought to be bad for the digestion if eaten at night – something people won't hesitate to tell you if you're foolhardy enough to try ordering one of them for supper.

Week ending

The Andalucians are highly social creatures, and multi-generational meal times, often outside, are very much part of the culture. On Sundays in particular, families head for the beach or the countryside. Some cook *paella* – there are special parks for people to do this; others head for restaurants that are specifically geared to the family.

Do check out the *ventas*, wayside establishments where travellers have been eating and sleeping since Don Quixote's time. The best way to choose one is to follow the crowds and pick one with an overflowing car park. The food will be no-nonsense hearty fare, though some will have their own specialities. Keep an eye on what others are ordering, because often there isn't a menu. You should also try *chiringuitos*, or beach bars, which may be anything from a temporary hut to an establishment with linen tablecloths. Lots of these places serve really excellent, freshly caught fish and seafood. With popular venues you can expect to have to queue for a table in summer – but this is hardly a chore when you are already on the beach.

After dark

Naturally enough, on a very hot day after a large lunch washed down with some lovely wine, a siesta is essential. Partake of this, and you will find yourself progressing easily towards the reviving evening stroll – perhaps in search of a sherry and a tapa – at around 9pm.

Proper sit-down dinners are available too, of course, although for the Spanish this does tend to be the least important meal of the day: one of the reasons why tapas are so popular. On the other hand, when you're on holiday, things are different. For a start, calories don't really count, do they; and if you've just spent the day striding out across the sierras, or slogging round the chic boutiques of Seville, or even cooling off in the pool, then you may consider an evening meal to be absolutely *de rigueur*, or *imprescindible*, as the Spanish say. You could even do the lot: a siesta, an early-ish tapa (not too early, though), a late-ish supper, and then the late-late nightcap ... you're here on holiday, after all.

Anyway, whatever you decide to do, you'll want to enjoy it. So here are some of the places I think you'll really have fun checking out – province by province.

Restaurants

There are thousands and thousands of restaurants in Andalucía, some of them incredibly good, some of them very ordinary. Whole books can be (and have been) devoted to giving you the details of all of them. In this section my aim is just to give you a tiny taste of the wide range of *Andaluz* eating experiences that are on offer – from *haute cuisine* to *menú del día*, from ducal palace to roadside café.

Opening times: a word to the wise

Spanish restaurant opening hours tend to be a law unto themselves. By and large, a restaurant won't open for lunch before one o'clock, and it's more likely to be one-thirty or even later. In Andalucía, most people will take lunch from about two or two-thirty onwards. It's quite common to see people still lunching at four, and even later on Sundays.

Similarly, in the evenings, places won't open much before eight-thirty. In the cities and at weekends, in fact, no-one really sits down to eat before ten-thirty, and it's quite unremarkable to be starting your dinner at midnight. In quiet or rural areas, though, things usually get going much earlier, and some places will even be closing by ten.

Many restaurants and bars will be closed on Sunday nights, and usually on another night in the week too – most commonly on Mondays, but not invariably. Do phone and check for details before making a long trek.

Cádiz

Almería province

El Almajero **

Located right on the harbour front, this well-known fish restaurant has an attractive terrace where you can watch the fishing boats unload their catch. It's no surprise the owners boast your meal comes "straight from the sea to the table" and they won't open if they think the fish isn't sufficiently good quality. Everything on the menu is excellent: sea bream, Garruchan red prawns, red mullet and haddock (from Norway) feature regularly, along with seafood casserole, seafood rice and mixed fish grill.

Puerto de Garrucha s/n, Garrucha
Tel: 950 460 405

La Terraza de Carmona ***

This hotel has the best restaurant and tapas bar for miles around. They specialise in local dishes such as *las torticas de Avio de Vera*, a kind of pizza made with maize flour and topped off with tomatoes, onion, fresh anchovy, herbs and olive oil; *ajo colorado*, which here is made with skate (not salt-cod), potatoes and paprika; desserts include one invented by the local convent called *la tarta borracha* or drunken cake. Their wine list is huge, with a big selection not just from Spain but also Chile, California and South Africa.

C Manuel Giménez 1, Vera
Tel: 950 390 760

Cádiz province

Bar Las Bridas **

Owner Manuel Sierra Pérez is the kind of chap who will send you away if you appear before 10pm when he isn't yet ready for his customers. And he won't open at all if the seas have been too rough to go fishing that day: yesterday's fish is never on the menu here. His establishment is something of an anomaly: a restaurant that serves tapas, or *raciones* (larger portions) to be exact, for diners to share. There isn't a menu, so the waiter recites what is available, which is usually served griddled, *a la plancha*. The quality of both the fish and the cooking is fantastic – tender squid, light and crispy John Dory goujons (think fish fingers for grown-ups) and, for the more adventurous, whole hake roes. These look like small sausages, have a grainy texture and delicate fishy taste. If you have been put off fish roes by the experience of putrid pink Greek taramasalata, do try these – they're delicious. And if Señor Pérez happens to like you, you'll be given his potato salad too.

Paseo de la Rosaleda 4, Jerez
Tel: 956 304 566

Cádiz El Chico *

Come here to eat no-nonsense grub. Dishes regularly featuring on the menu include Grazalema cheese and charcuterie, *sopa de Grazalema* (broth with ham, bread and chopped-up hard-boiled egg), roast leg of young lamb, venison in red wine, and wild boar.

Plaza de España 8, Grazalema
Tel: 956 132 027

Casa Bigote **

When you visit Sanlúcar de Barrameda head for the Bajo de Guía and discover for yourself why people rave about the combination of *manzanilla* and seafood. Bars and restaurants line the waterfront of this attractive town and you can experience top quality fish washed down with the freshest, fabulous fortified wine. The eateries are all very good and everyone has their own particular favourite venue but Casa Bigote is one of our favourites. Come here to drool over their sea bream dish, *urta a la roteña*, excellent tuna belly and the totally heavenly Sanlúcar langoustines. Mantis prawns are also available in spring and here they make a soup with them called *sopa de galeras*. The restaurant has a comprehensive range of manzanillas and you shouldn't leave without trying their home-made moscatel and raisin ice cream with Pedro Ximénez poured over the top. The waiter just leaves the bottle on the table for you to add as much as you want.

Bajo de Guía 10, Sanlúcar de Barrameda
Tel: 956 362 696

Casa José María **

An excellent seafood restaurant, with wonderful tuna and a wide range of other dishes including shellfish, seafood and rice dishes, *pescado a la sal* (fish cooked under salt), and, for the more adventurous, cod with cream of sea urchin. The beef and lamb

served up here is good too, just in case anyone should feel they are developing gills from all the fish they've been eating.

Plaza Márques de Tamarón, Zahara de los Atunes
Tel: 956 439 338

Casa Juan **

This is regularly mentioned in the guide books for a good reason: it has a great terrace overlooking the river and, most importantly, dishes up great food. Absolutely not to be missed is their house special of prawn rice or *arroz con langostinos*. Actually the langoustines on their own are wonderful too.

Bajo de Guía 26, Sanlúcar de Barrameda
Tel: 956 362 695

El Campero **

Although they serve other locally-caught fish, this restaurant specialises in tuna from the almadraba, served in a variety of different

ways. There's *mojama* (salt-cured tuna), smoked tuna, tuna roe, tuna heart, sashimi and just about every possible cut of tuna you can think of.

Av de la Constitución, Local 5c, Barbate
Tel: 956 432 300

El Convento **

This is a fairly formal old-style restaurant situated in the patio of a seventeenth-century palace. It's well-known for cooking local traditional dishes such as *berza de tagarninas* (thistle stew), *sopa de esparragos* (wild asparagus soup), *conejo de monte en arroz* (mountain rabbit with rice), and *perdiz en salsa de almendras* (partridge in almond sauce). It also has a selection of unusual puddings: particularly delicious is the Moorish-influenced dessert *jalea de naranjas* (fresh orange jelly).

C Márques de Torresto 7, Arcos de la Frontera
Tel: 956 703 233

Arcos de la Frontera

El Faro **

For many people, this is probably the best restaurant in the city. It feels a bit like an English club – of the large white crisp linen napkin variety. It does great shellfish, paella, traditional stews and seafood salads. It's not cheap, but they also do a set lunch menu, which is good value.

C San Felix 15, Cádiz
Tel: 956 211 068

El Ventorillo El Chato *

This historic posthouse is just outside the city and dates from the end of the eighteenth century. It serves excellent local fish including tuna and sea bream, along with fishy stews and rice dishes.

Ctra Cádiz-San Fernando km 2
Tel: 956 250 025

Hacienda de Rosalejo **

Set in a beautiful refurbished eighteenth-century ducal palace with surrounding gardens, this restaurant is the place to visit when you fancy something a bit special. The soups are especially good: try *sopa de almendras* (almond soup) or *crema fría de puerro con bacon frito y aceite de cebollino* (cold cream of leek with fried bacon and chive oil). The *magret de pato y salsa moscatel* (duck magret and moscatel wine sauce) is wonderful, too.

Ctra Villamartin-Ubrique km 6.6
Tel: 956 231 000

Hotel Hurricane **

This hotel's evening-only restaurant is well-known in the area. It serves very good, locally-caught fish including tuna, sea bass, red bream and red porgy. Another reason for visiting is the excellent view across to the Moroccan coast.

Ctra N-340, km 77, Tarifa
Tel: 956 684 919

La Despensa **

This restaurant, which looks out onto the Atlantic Ocean, serves local cuisine in an innovative style. One of the best dishes is *turbantes de lubina* (literally, sea-bass turbans): rolled-up filleted fish are stuffed with asparagus paté and prawns, and then served with a hollandaise sauce. Another good fish dish is gilt-head bream steak stuffed with salmon, and served with a cava sauce. It really makes you want to book a table now.

C Escritor Ramón Solís 9-10, Cádiz
Tel: 956 265 320

Córdoba province

El Churrasco **

This is one of the best restaurants in Córdoba, frequented by tourists and locals alike. There's a tapas bar at the front, while to the rear is an attractive patio, its walls festooned in ivy and ceramic plates. The menu, as the name implies, is strong on grilled meats, such as a terrific rib of beef from Valles de los Pedroches, but there are lots of other things to choose from. Typical starters are white gazpacho with pine nuts or a salmorejo that's lava-thick with plenty of diced ham and crumbled boiled egg – almost a meal in itself. The scrambled eggs with prawns, *revuelto con gambas*, is a popular choice with lunching Spaniards. For main courses, grilled duck breast with date salsa is an unusual variation on the old duck-and-orange combo. And the puddings are great: try the gin and tonic ice cream with lemon sorbet.

C Romero 16, Judería, Córdoba
Tel: 957 290 819

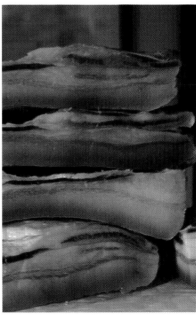

Las Camachas *

This is a popular large hacienda just outside Montilla. You can either stick with tapas in the attractive tiled bar, or choose one of six dining areas. Regional specialities include *alcachofas al Montilla* (artichokes braised in Montilla wine), *salmorejo* (creamy gazpacho), and *cordero a la miel de Jara* (lamb in honey). You can also buy local wines here.

Antigua Ctra Córdoba-Málaga, Montilla
Tel: 957 650 004

Granada province

Bar Peña *

Just about everybody who lives in Alcudia drops in at some point during the day to the Bar Peña for something to eat and a drink – and a chat with Paca, the very friendly owner. The food is good, simple, Andalucian home cooking. There is no official *menú del día* but the style of eating (and the prices) are definitely along those lines: a daily *potaje* (soupy vegetable stew) or similar, followed by a meat or fish dish, a salad if you want it, and then a dessert. Choose between a carafe of Per-Sot rosé, a locally-produced wine, or a bottle of Rioja. Paca also does special requests: order what you want, a meal or two in advance, and she will cook it for you, whether you fancy migas with all the trimmings, or perhaps even goat stew. She can also have the food ready for you at times that are very un-Andalucian: great if you've got hungry children who can't hang on till nine at night to have supper. At weekends Paca lights up a charcoal grill and serves up tapas of grilled pork slices, chorizos and black puddings. The restaurant area is small and it can get busy, but there are also tables and chairs outside.

Ctra de Almería km 1, Alcudia de Guadix
Tel: 958 698 033

Bar-Quesería Rossini *

In summer you can sit outside on the terrace, while in winter you should aim for a fireside table on one of two floors to sample Manolo Rossini's boards of sliced cheeses, cured meats, patés and smoked foods. He has a large range of gourmet specialities in his chill cabinet, many produced locally in the province of Granada or elsewhere in Andalucía: goat's cheese from the small town of Montefrío, black pudding and cured sausage from villages around the city of Granada, fried pork loin preserved in olive oil (from Jaén) or lard (from Ronda). Barranco Oscuro, a fruity red produced on the high slopes of the Alpujarras, is one of the many Spanish wines available.

Campo de Príncipe 15, Granada
Tel: 958 228 227

Bar Terraza Manolo *

A village bar and restaurant that draws people from quite a way around because of its wonderful *latas de cordero*: deep roasting tins of Segureño lamb and potatoes, cooked in a hot oven. Other specialities of the house are couscous with black pudding and migas. Manolo produces his own rosé wine, which makes an excellent accompaniment to the locally-produced lamb. You will find that a simple lettuce, tomato and onion salad (which is all you need to follow the generous portions of lamb) tastes better here than in other places. This, according to Manolo, is because all the ingredients are grown locally. There are three dining areas: a small back dining room (with a fireplace for winter eating), the bar area, and a very pleasant outdoor terrace. However, you still need to order your lamb in advance (ringing in the morning on the day you want to eat is usually fine).

C Iglesia 1, Galera
Tel: 958 739 165

Casa El Cepillo *

This small and always packed restaurant is situated beside the outdoor stalls of Granada's busy fruit and vegetable market. It offers cheap and basic fare but is one of the best places to get a *menú del día* in the city, as the food is cooked with locals and not tourists in mind. You'll need to get there early, though, as there is nearly always a queue of hungry diners waiting by the door.

Plaza Pescadería 8, Granada
Tel: none!

Cunini ***

Cunini is an elegant fish restaurant and tapas bar that's been going nearly 55 years. Here, your first drink comes with a free tapa of *migas con sardinas*; if you stay for a second drink you'll be given a portion of delicious paella-like rice with fish and seafood. You can then order a variety of other fishy tapas, including oysters. For something more substantial, try the two-person *parillada de pescados y mariscos*, which consists of grilled prawns, king prawns, mussels, turbot, salmon, monkfish and swordfish. Forget sightseeing in the afternoon.

Plaza Pescadería 14, Granada
Tel: 958 250 777

L'Atelier **

L'Atelier is a charmingly quirky vegetarian guesthouse and restaurant in Mecina Fondales, high in the Alpujarras. Owner Jean-Claude Juston's award-winning food is a fusion of Moroccan, Asian and Spanish influences, using fresh organic produce, sourced locally. Dinner on one cold and starry night included maize and peanut croquettes served sizzling straight from the pan; an Indonesian-style salad of grapes,

pineapple and spinach glistening with freshness and an unctuous peanut butter sauce; a carrot and coriander soup; and a *parmentier* – a spicy cottage pie with ginger and fresh thyme. Desserts included favourites like chocolate mousse and a wickedly rich chocolate bombe, and an unusual but delicious pastry with almonds and poppy seeds. L'Atelier also offers vegetarian cookery courses, and there's a discount for members of vegetarian organizations. A share of the profits goes to benefit street children in Colombia, too.

C Alberca s/n, Mecina Fondales
Tel: 958 857 501

López Correa *

This Granadine institution began life in the 1890s as a distillery and a bodega for selling wines. By the early 1980s it had become a tiny bar with room enough for just a few people to stand, where you could order a

glass of local wine, *vino de la costa*, and still get change from the equivalent of 20p. It was hugely popular: three tapas would arrive with a drink – half a hard-boiled egg with a dollop of mayonnaise, a handful of peanuts, and a piece of sausage. These days it's only the one *tapa*, but the grandchildren of Señor López Correa have opened up the behind-the-counter area so that customers can sit and sample an excellent-value *menú del día* that uses only the best local produce. Everything is home-made, from the meatballs to the custard pudding. *Plato Alpujarreño*, a dish from the nearby Alpujarras region with black pudding and chorizo, potato and peppers, makes a frequent appearance on the menu, as does rabbit with rice. If you are there in spring or early summer, a good choice is the wild asparagus soup.

C Molinos 5, Granada
Tel: 958 222 351

Restaurante Cuevas Pedro Antonio de Alarcón **

A very friendly family-run cave restaurant, attached to the nearby cave hotel, and serving traditional Andalucian cuisine as well as more unusual dishes (some of which need to be ordered in advance). The roast lamb with almonds, raisins and honey is delicious, as are the lamb chops with rosemary and thyme, and the roast rabbit. Portions are large and the dining room gets very busy. There are some tables outside. After eating you can take a stroll around the troglodyte neighbourhood of the restaurant, where you will spot chimneys poking out of the ground, or go into the centre of Guadix, a town with a tradition of cave-dwelling going back to the 1400s – and where still today some 10,000 people live in caves.

Barriada San Torcuato, Guadix
Tel: 958 664 986

Rincón de Yegen **

A small hotel with a very good restaurant, and well worth making a note of, as good restaurants are rather thin on the ground round here. The chef and proprietor, Agustín Rodríguez, who runs the Rincón with his wife Mari Carmen, is careful to pick good local foods and produce, and is almost apologetic when something isn't home-made: "We don't actually make the black pudding ourselves, but it is made very close to here," he explains. One of Agustín's specialities is fresh home-made noodles with toasted almonds and garlic, a local tradition. Salt-cod with peppers, tomatoes and aubergines is another speciality of the house. There are some nice Riojas on the wine list, and also a selection of local Alpujarran wines from bodegas like Cuatro Vientos and Barranco Oscuro. Yegen was the village where the English writer Gerald Brenan lived in the 1920s and 1930s, visited by Virginia Woolf and Lytton Strachey. You can walk off your lunch with a stroll around the village, or on one of the longer walks connected with Brenan around the Yegen countryside.

Camino de Gerald Brenan s/n, Yegen
Tel: 958 851 270

Huelva province

Casa Rufino ***

Considered by some to be the best restaurant along the Huelva coastline, the Rufino's seafood and rice dishes are very good, as is the tuna. The place is famous for its tasting menu, known as *el tonteo*, which consists of eight different fish dishes. A minimum of 4 people is needed to order this.

Av de la Playa Central s/n, Isla Cristina
Tel: 959 330 810

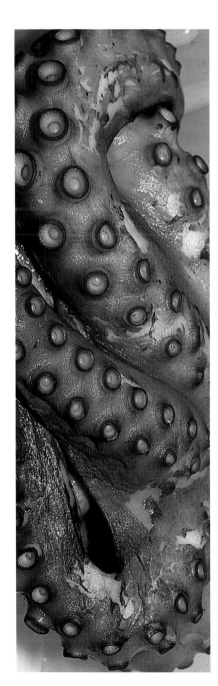

El Paraíso *

Quite a large restaurant, set amongst pine trees and very close to the beach. It's well-known locally for the quality and freshness of its seafood. The *coquinas* (clams) and the white prawns are heaven on a plate, and the fish, which is served a la plancha, is always excellent.

Ctra Huelva-El Portíl km 15.5
Tel: 959 312 756

El Rompido is an attractive fishing town (in spite of some recent development) and has a collection of restaurants situated in the fishermen's quarter. Everything is, of course, fresh that day, and in general it's no-nonsense fare: fried fish of all kinds, shellfish, griddled fish and fish stews are what people come here to eat. A dish that is very popular is called *calamares del campo*, literally, squid from the countryside, which are in fact deep-fried pepper and onion rings.

Jaén province

Parador de Úbeda **

This splendid parador is a converted sixteenth-century ducal palace. The restaurant is open to non-residents and specialises in regional dishes, with partridge featuring strongly: the stuffed green peppers are delicious, as is the stewed partridge with plums; otherwise you can opt for a simple marinaded partridge salad. Meat dishes include bull's tail in red wine sauce, and stewed kid with pine nuts.

Plaza Vázquez de Molina s/n, Úbeda
Tel: 953 750 345

Vandelvira ***

The restaurant is located in two galleries on the first floor of the Convento de San Francisco, overlooking the patio. It's decorated in a formal but baroque Spanish style, with lots of heavy antiques and huge red velvet curtains. Again partridge is the chef's favoured bird. Specialities include the *paté de perdiz con aceite de oliva virgen* (partridge paté with olive oil) or the *manitas de cerdo rellenas de perdiz y espinacas* (pig's knuckles filled with partridge and spinach).

C San Francisco 14, Baeza
Tel: 953 748 172

Málaga province

Casa Juan *

This is a traditional restaurant serving fish and shellfish which is very popular at Sunday lunchtime. As is typical of this kind of establishment, there are few frills, as the fish comes first: they have been serving the same dishes, always prepared in the same way, for decades, to suit their gastronomically conservative regulars. And thank goodness for that.

C Río Rocío 10, Huelin
Tel: 952 325 211

Caserío de San Benito **

This restaurant is well worth a detour – it's special for several reasons. In winter you eat inside in a cosy farmhouse-style dining room, and in summer tables are laid outside, among geraniums and huge earthenware jars. There's a marvellous chapel-like museum in the grounds, too. You'll find good local dishes on the menu: the *ajo blanco* (cold almond and garlic soup), served with chopped apple and raisins, is delicious, as is the soupy rabbit with rice. On the dessert menu is *bienmesabe*, a fabulously sweet brown confection of angel's-hair pumpkin, almonds, eggs, sugar and cinnamon. On the wine list you'll find a red Gadea and a white Montespejo from nearby Mollina; both are worth a try. The service is friendly and informal. Closed July 1-20; also closed Tuesday, Wednesday and Thursday evenings in the winter months.

Ctra de Córdoba-Málaga km 108, Antequera
Tel: 952 034 000

El Vegetariano de Alcazabilla *

A really idiosyncratic restaurant, El Vegetariano does some wonderful things with local vegetables. The walls are graffitied with literally thousands of comments from happy diners glad to have found a veggie treat in a very meaty province. A *menú del día* costs €8 and will set you up for the rest of the day's sightseeing in Málaga's rapidly regenerating old quarters.

C Pozo del Rey 5, Málaga
Tel: 952 214 858

Hotel Cerro de Híjar **

Here the chefs take traditional dishes and give them a modern twist. For example, humble oxtail stew is transformed into sublime ravioli where the meat is wrapped up in wafer-thin rice pasta sheets, while gravy has been elevated to *jus*. Rabbit casserole is given similar treatment. Vegetarians meanwhile can enjoy grilled local goat's cheese salad or big meaty wild mushrooms that are grilled and then coated in a garlic, olive oil and parsley purée. And why not stay the night? After all, this is a hotel restaurant – and then you can go for a walk in the sierras the next morning to work off your indulgence.

Cerro de Híjar s/n, Tolox
Tel: 952 112 111

Mesón La Molienda **

This extremely popular restaurant and bar was set up as a co-operative by a group of local people who wanted to carry on living in their lovely village and not have to look for jobs on the Costa del Sol. La Molienda now employs quite a lot of villagers, not only in the restaurant but also in their new food shop. You can sit outside on the patio or in one of several eating areas inside. Do try and choose a spot near a window, as Benalauría is high up in the sierras and the views are superb. On the menu are unusual starters like a hot gazpacho, and salads of orange or lettuce with mint (grown here ever since the village was inhabited by Moors). Second courses include some delicious stews – lamb with almonds or with chestnuts (another local crop: they appear on the dessert menu, too). In early August there is a re-enactment of a battle in the village: a very colourful spectacle, after which vast numbers of people head back to La Molienda for drinks and lunch. It is obviously essential to book for that day, as it is for most weekends.

C Moraleda 59, Benalauría
Tel: 952 152 548

Mesón La Salina **

Unpretentious, rustic and no-nonsense, this is reckoned to be one of the best *mesones* in the province. It's the sort of place Columbus might have gone for dinner with the king and queen, and little appears to have changed since then, although doctors, lawyers and foreigners have now replaced the old Spanish nobility at the tables. The menu is dominated by classic meat dishes such as *solomillo escándalo* – beef with a rich red wine, cinnamon, clove and allspice sauce. Of equal importance is the wine list, and La Salina's list of over 200 claims to feature the 30 best wines in Spain. Be careful with that credit card: who could resist a Pingus 2001, at €700?

Av La Salina 28, Los Boliches, Fuengirola
Tel: 952 471 806

Restaurante La Espuela **

An oasis of calm in a very noisy town, and if you have just done millennia-old Antequera with all its historic monuments (more per square mile than anywhere else in Spain), then you may be grateful to have the chance to sit down and eat relatively early. The *menu típico* is a good choice: *porra antequerana*, the thick dip-like version of gazpacho which is a speciality of the town; slowly stewed bull's tail cooked with rosemary-scented honey; followed by a pudding. This menu comes with a glass of the red house wine, Serres, which is a Rioja. On the à la carte menu are dishes such as partridge paté drizzled with rabbit oil, and roast leg of lamb. La Espuela also serves good pizzas – ideal for keeping hungry children quiet while the adults savour the excellent food and wine.
A small word of warning: the restaurant moved from its old address in the bullring several years ago, but many guidebooks still list it with the wrong directions.
C San Agustín 1, Antequera
Tel: 952 703 031

Salón de Pescado *

This opened as a small fish restaurant in 1978 with fish piled in platters on the counter and cooked to order. They now have an elegantly decorated two-storey place across the road, still displaying the day's catch on trays, but cooking in a large kitchen that opens onto the restaurant. José, the affable owner, will happily describe the fish available that day and detail some of the specialities of the house such as monkfish.
Not surprisingly, it's very busy at the weekends.
C Las Navas 18-32, Huelin
Tel: 952 332 862

Willy Moya

Tierra del Fuego *

This is a gourmet vegetarian restaurant run by Paul and Julia, whose aim is to show that the richness of Spanish vegetables and fruit can be served in an exciting and fresh way. While not typically Andalucian, the region's connection with its Moorish past is clearly visible: filo parcels with goat's cheese, walnuts and herbs is a delicious example; or couscous cake with feta and pine nuts, served with spinach, spices and roasted red peppers. The decor is typically Spanish with Granadine tiles and simple Spanish chairs and white walls.
Edificio Córdoba, Av Tore Tore 16, Torre del Mar
Tel: 952 546 414

Seville province

Egaña Oriza ***

This is one of Seville's most stylish restaurants, situated in the conservatory of a restored mansion, next door to the Murillo Gardens. Food served here is actually Basque-inspired, as that is where owner-chef José Mari Egaña comes from. He combines his passion for hunting with cooking, and his game is sourced from within Andalucía. The seasonal menu varies: in winter you could be in luck with woodcock flamed in Spanish brandy, or casserole of wild boar with cherries and raisins.
C San Fernando 41, Seville
Tel: 954 227 211

Poncio ***

Enthusiastic and dynamic chef Willy Moya trained in Paris and now reinterprets Andalucian dishes in a modern style. Everything here is delicious: his white gazpacho with a ball of melon and ham sorbet is heaven in a soup bowl. The

Tapas bars

Eating tapas

There is a splendid legend that tapas were invented by a barman parking a slice of bread over a glass of wine to keep the flies off. True or not, tapas indubitably suit the gregarious way the Spanish like to eat, and they are the ideal solution to apartment living in towns and cities that can get horribly hot in summer. Imagine attempting to give supper parties when it is 45 degrees. Quite sensibly, the Spanish just don't do it: if they want to see their friends, they simply go out, rather late at night by northern European standards, once the temperatures have started to cool down.

What makes the tapas experience so special here is the Andalucian attitude to it. The food, wonderful as it may be, still plays second fiddle to the good time you are having with your friends. And unlike the rest of the world, where wine is seen as an accompaniment to food, here in Andalucía the tiny plates of food are, if anything, a supporting cast to the drinks. But the *tapeo* is no British pub-crawl, by any means, and the aim of this particular game is certainly not to get legless: drunken behaviour is seriously uncool in Spain.

Tapas traditions vary across the region. In Jaén and Granada, for example, beer is the favoured tipple, and the tapa that accompanies your drink is free. The fun bit (or the worry, depending on how adventurous you're feeling) is that there's no choice of tapa – the delicious, and occasionally enigmatic, morsel that is delivered to you is a complete surprise. You may hear the waiter shouting towards the kitchen *un primero!* or *un segundo!*, to let the kitchen know which tapa to prepare, but you'll just have to wait and see what it turns

out to be. The upshot of this is that people will often order another round just to find out what the next tapa is. Now, if you were drinking a glass of wine, or a half of lager, every time you did this, then you'd soon be over the limit. Consequently, the beer served here isn't particularly alcoholic, and it's served in a small glass too.

In Almería, customers are even allowed to choose their free tapas. On the western side of the region, by contrast, all your tapas will typically have to be paid for – but of course you can choose what you'd like.

Some visitors to Andalucía tend to go out a bit too early in the evening, hoping to find a great array of tapas, and they're likely to be disappointed, because the kitchens don't really gear up properly until at least nine or ten at night. On the whole, the bars don't give too much thought to decor, because their customers don't either, but they are enormously competitive about their tapas, which are their main method of keeping their customers loyal: a bar's most faithful clientele will generally be given larger than standard portions, you'll notice.

Tapas aren't just a nocturnal activity, by the way. They're also popular for lunch, where you'll often see groups of workers settling down to a meze-style collection of tapas.

The times they are a-changing, though, and habits from northern Europe have gradually begun to erode this typically Spanish custom, and there are signs too that Spaniards are going out less in the evening for tapas, especially during the week. "We should have spainified Europe, not europeanised Spain," grumbled one tapas bar owner from Granada, contemplating the prospect of having to find a second job.

aubergine *cortadillo* is a double-decker sandwich of aubergine, goat's cheese and salmorejo with raisins and crumbled hard-boiled egg. Carnivores can drool over lamb roasted in a wood-burning oven; while fish lovers will wax lyrical about the salt-baked sea bass served with prawn oil and olive caviar. The grilled squid is gorgeous too – served with a green gazpacho of spinach, basil and mint, and grilled veg. There are à la carte and set menus, which are only in Spanish, and the restaurant keeps very Spanish time (opening at 2pm for lunch and 9pm for dinner): this place is geared to pleasing a local crowd. But the charming Maitre d', named Omar (his mum had a thing about the actor), not only speaks very good English, he will happily recommend wines for every course you choose.

C Victoria 8, Seville
Tel: 954 340 010

Spot a winner

Confused by the huge range of tapas bars to choose from? Well, the best way to pick a winner is to check out the floor – if there's a lot of litter and mess by the bar, then you're probably in for a treat. Whether it's a lovely old classic tiled bar or a modern trendy one with minimalist decor, the custom is still to eat tapas standing at the bar and to drop the remains directly onto the floor. Prawn shells, olive stones, cocktail sticks, paper napkins, snail shells, all are discarded, to be swept up later. So, the more mess there is, the more popular the establishment must be.

Some bars will specialise in certain types of tapas – deep-fried fish and seafood, say – or be known for one speciality that the cooks do particularly well. Many regular tapas-trailers have their own set routes, taking in the bars that serve their favourite tapas. You'll find several places where the tapas are laid out on the counter. But many only serve food freshly to order – and the names are often chalked up in long lists on boards, which can make things a bit tricky if you don't speak much Spanish. The secret is to look around at what other people are eating, and, when ordering, don't be afraid to point.

The tapas trail

The experience of strolling from bar to bar, grazing on tapas and sipping at sherry, is unique to Spain. Somehow, other nations' interpretation of it seems to lose something in translation, because if you go to a tapas bar in London or New York, the chances are you'll stay put for the evening. Not so in Spain, and certainly not in Andalucía. Part of the art of tapas is exploring the trail. So enjoy a tapa or two at one bar, then pay your tab, which is often chalked up on the counter in front of you, and then venture forth to seek out another. And Seville, as it happens, is a great place to start venturing forth into.

Tapas A-Z

There are hundreds of traditional *tapas* which are perennially popular. Here are just a few of them:

Aceitunas: olives, marinaded in vinegar, often with an addition of garlic, herbs and spices. The word *aceituna* is from Arabic, but Spanish also uses *oliva*, from Latin.

Albóndigas: meatballs. These are frequently made from pork and served in a tomato or almond based sauce.

Almejas: clams. These are often served in a white wine based sauce. *Chirlas* are baby clams.

Boquerones: fresh anchovies, served marinaded or deep fried. This is also the nickname given to people from Málaga, because of their partiality for the large *boquerones Victorianos*, from Rincón de la Victoria.

Berenjenas: aubergines, which are sometimes fried with honey, a dish that goes back to the times of the Moors.

Bacalao: cod, either fresh or salted, served as a tapa in thousands of ways:

bacalao con tomate, cod in tomato sauce, is a classic recipe.

Calamares a la romana: deep-fried squid rings.

Callos: stewed tripe.

Caracoles: snails – frequently served in a spicy sauce.

Carne en salsa: stewed meat in sauce.

Carne mechada: fried seasoned meat.

Cazón en adobo: dogfish, marinaded and then deep-fried.

Champiñones al ajillo: garlic mushrooms.

Chorizo: sausage, sliced, fried or cooked in wine (*al vino*).

Coquinas: clams.

Croquetas: croquettes – can be made with cod, potato or ham.

Ensalada malagueña: a popular Málaga salad made from salt-cod, oranges, olives onion and potato.

Ensaladilla rusa: Russian salad (vegetables in mayonnaise).

Espinacas con garbanzos: spinach with chickpeas, a popular Sevillian tapa.

Flamenquines: ham or veal in breadcrumbs, deep-fried.

Fritos: a general term for deep-fried tapas.

Gambas: prawns.

Gambas rebozadas: prawns in breadcrumbs, deep-fried.

Gambas al ajillo: garlicky prawns.

Gambas a la gabardina: prawns in overcoats, that is, deep-fried in batter.

Habas con jamón: broad beans with serrano ham.

Huevo cocido: a hard-boiled egg (which usually comes with a salt pot).

Jamón serrano: dry-cured ham. A *taco de jamón* is a small thickly-cut piece of ham.

Jamón ibérico: dry-cured ham made from acorn-fed pigs.

Langostinos: langoustines usually served *a la plancha*.

Lomo en orza: pork loin preserved in oil.

Mejillones: mussels.

Migas: fried breadcrumbs.

Mojama: salt-cured tuna.

Morcilla: black pudding.

Navajas: razor clams.

Patatas bravas: fried chunks of potato in a chilli sauce and also, sometimes, garlic mayonnaise.

Pincho moruno: marinaded pork pieces grilled on a skewer.

Papas: a word used in southern Spain for potatoes or crisps.

Patatas alioli: chunks of potato in garlic mayonnaise.

Pescaito frito: also called *pescado frito* – deep-fried small fish.

Picadillo de chorizo: chorizo sausage-meat, fried.

Pisto: peppers, courgette, onion and tomato, fried in olive oil.

Pringá: a classic Sevillian tapa of cooked meats from a cocido, served without the chickpeas and vegetables (see page 76 for more details).

Pulpo: octopus, tenderised and then boiled; frequently served chopped up with onion and tomato as a salad.

Puntas puntillitas: or *puntitas de calamar* – deep-fried baby squid.

Queso: cheese, which often comes with a piece of bread and a few olives.

Remojón: a salad made with cod and oranges.

Riñones al jerez: kidneys in sherry sauce.

Salchichón: cured salami-type sausage.

Salpicón de mariscos: a chilled seafood salad in a vinaigrette dressing.

Sepia: cuttlefish

Soldadito de pavia: salt-cod fingers, deep-fried; a popular tapa from Seville.

Tortilla española: potato omelette, which has always been a favourite with everyone. These days it's getting harder to find a really good, classic, four centimetre thick *tortilla* as it requires slow, patient cooking – but Andalucía is one region of Spain where they still have bus stations (which, strangely, always seem to serve great tortillas).

Tortilla de camarones: very small prawns, made into round crispy batter fritters.

What's in a name?

Some tapas terminology to watch out for:

Montadito is a tapa with a bread base and a topping. In Andalucía this is likely to be local *salchichón*, or *jamón* or cheese or something freshly cooked *a la plancha* – perhaps a slice of pork loin, or a chunk of *morcilla* or some *panceta*. There are hundreds of Andalucian variations on the montadito, as there are on another small tapa:

Bocadillo, which also refers to a sort of bread or bread roll with a topping or a filling. Some bars even have their own invented names for their bread-based tapas, just to confuse you: *pitufillo*, *jarapillo*, *rellenito*, *chicuco de almacén* and *rosquillo* are just some of the names you may come across.

Banderilla is a tapa on a cocktail stick

Brocheta or **pinchito** is a hot tapa on a skewer

Cazuela is a dish cooked and served in a small earthenware bowl

Tabla is a wooden board, usually with a selection of cheeses or porky bits.

Tapas also come in different-sized servings, although they may not all be available: a *tapa* is the smallest-sized serving, followed by a *media ración*; the largest is a *ración*, which is more or less a plateful.

Seville tapas

North-east of the cathedral

Bodeguita Entrecarceles – which literally means "between jails" – only opens in the evenings. This is a good place to come if you want to try out some of the more elusive boutique sherries, as they offer a good range by the glass.

C Manuel Cortina 3

El Rinconcillo was established in 1670 and prides itself as the longest established tapas bar in the city. It certainly has bags of character, with elaborately tiled walls and shelves of bottles racked to the ceilings. There is a good range of sherries to try, ranging from famous brands like Tío Pepe to the less well-known Manzanilla Pavón. Sample classic tapas such as chickpeas and spinach, and salt-cod with tomato. The barmen will chalk your tab on the counter in front of you, in the traditional way.

C Gerona 40

A glass of something with your tapas?

Sherry

The classic accompaniment to tapas in Andalucía is a glass of chilled sherry – *una copa de fino* or *de manzanilla*, or simply *un fino* or *una manzanilla* (but if you're asking for the latter, make sure that the waiter doesn't think you want a cup of camomile tea, which is also *manzanilla*; if in doubt, ask for *un vino de manzanilla*).

Other wines

If you ask for a *vino*, you will generally get a glass of ordinary red wine, and likewise if you ask for a *tinto*. For a white wine, ask for a *vino blanco*, and if you want something better than plonk then ask for it by name or region. A *mosto* is a good accompaniment to tapas – this is a chilled local rosé wine that is not bottled but is served from a wine box or a carafe on the bar counter. *Sangria* may be the wine-based drink that most people associate with Spain, but in Andalucía you'll find that *tinto de verano*, red wine diluted with lemonade, is very popular; while *rebujito* is a fiesta favourite – sherry diluted with lemonade.

Beer

Lager-style beer is always a popular accompaniment to *tapas* in Andalucía. Cruzcampo is a very good beer, made in Seville. In terms of what to ask for, *un tubo* is the term frequently used in the region for a tall glass of draught beer; and *una caña* is the term for a small glass. Bottled beers come in two sizes: *un quinto* is the smaller, and refers to a bottle of beer containing a fifth of a litre; *un tercio* is a bottle containing a third of a litre. An alcohol-free beer is *una cerveza sin alcohol*.

Soft drinks

Un refresco is the general term for a cold soft drink, but these are normally ordered by name, e.g. *una Fanta naranja* (an orange Fanta).

Mixers

Tapas can be a prelude to a meal, or they can be a meal in themselves. But either way, people will often end the evening at a bar with a coffee and a cubata, which is a spirit and a mixer of some sort: whisky and soda, brandy and coke, gin and tonic (don't forget to try the Málaga-made gin, Larios). *Cubata* is a corruption of Cuba Libre, the Cuban rum and coke cocktail which was popular in the War of Independence: Cubans weren't allowed to say Free Cuba, so they ordered the drink instead. Strong links with Cuba meant that people were soon ordering it in Spain as a show of solidarity.

Taberna Coloniales is well-known for its grilled meats served with a salsa: *solomillo al roquefort* is one of its signature tapas. The bar has tables outside and, when it's busy, you can put your name down for a table on a waiting list chalked up on the blackboard. Otherwise join the throng indoors.
Plaza del Cristo Burgos 19

Around the cathedral
Cervecería Giralda used to be a Moorish bathhouse, but is now one of the more stylish tapas bars in Seville. Despite its touristy location near the cathedral, it still manages to produce super food, including some modern dishes like courgette *timbales*, and salt-cod with squid ink.
C Mateos Gago 1

Around Plaza Nueva
Casablanca doesn't have a menu or even a blackboard with a list of tapas; instead you have to point and ask, in Spanish, for what you'd like. This can be a little tricky when the place is heaving and everyone is jostling for bar space, but the intrepid will be well rewarded, because the tiny kitchen rustles up the most delicious and unusual tapas, such as *tortilla al whisky* (potato omelette fried in olive oil with garlic cloves and a good dousing of whisky).
C Zaragoza 50

Enrique Becerra is a slightly smarter establishment than some others, being a restaurant as well as a tapas bar.
C Gamazo 2

La Flor de Toranzo began trading as a butcher's, before turning into a tapas bar specialising in cured meats about 50 years ago. Try their ibérico ham: it's excellent; and to accompany this, why not tipple on a Napoleon amontillado – it's produced by Vinicola Hidalgo, the bodega that also makes the best-selling Manzanilla La Gitana.
C Jimios 1 y 3, Joaquín 9

Arenal district

Bar Alfonso II is a straightforward neighbourhood bar, which the locals call King of the Snails, in deference to its speciality tapa.
C Santas Patronas 11

Cádiz tapas

As you meander round this little city, here are a few bars worth dropping into:

Bahía is a well-known bar serving tapas of typical local dishes.
C Ramón de Carranza 29

Bar Terraza is located in one of the most emblematic squares in Cádiz. It's a great place for fried fish with a glass of very cold fino.
Plaza de la Catedral s/n

El Balandro is a restaurant as well as a bar. It has great views across the bay to El Puerto de Santa María, and an extensive tapas list that changes frequently.
C Alameda Abodaca 22

Merodio is a fab little bar with great seafood tapas. Try the *tortillitas de camarones* (shrimp fritters) or *huevas* (fish roe).
C Libertad 4

Zapata serves excellent *montaditos* (mini toasted sandwiches) and *revueltos* (scrambled eggs).
Plaza de la Candelería s/n

And here are a few more tapas hotspots around the region:

Almería tapas

Casa Puga opened in 1870 and is still run by the same family. This is a very popular bar, considered by many to be the best in the city, and has lots of faithful regulars along with the occasional tourist. It is decorated with splendid blue tiles, and the rafters are crammed with dripping hams. There are around 80 tapas to choose from, as well as 40 or so raciones. Popular choices are marinaded anchovies, fried baby squid, grilled grouper and prawns in batter. Take your time choosing a wine: there are around 300 on the list.
C Jovellanos 7

Carzola tapas

Mesón Don Chema has a cavernous dining room, its walls lined with antelope heads and photos of hunting expeditions, so it's no surprise that this establishment specialises in game such as venison and boar. It's fun to squeeze in at the bar, TV blaring in one ear, and watch the tapas being rustled up in the tiny kitchen. The menu isn't huge, but consists of hearty morsels ideal for a chilly evening like *solomillo Don Chema* (deep-fried pork on bread with crispy fried peppers), *huevos a la Carzoleña* (eggs cooked in tomatoes, with loads of oil and potatoes), and trout marinaded *en escabeche*.
C Dr Muñoz s/n

Fuengirola tapas

Bar Esquina is a local tapas bar with *comedor* (dining area) that has been serving the local community for the last 19 years. It's also a prime example of where workers will be tucking into a simple, low-cost lunch to keep them going for the rest of the day, and this really is one of the best places to experience a typical Andalucian lunchtime. The *menú del día*, which includes wine and water, costs around €6.50, and is typically a lentil stew with bacon, or a mixed salad, followed by sardines or fried meat with potatoes, and finishing with fruit or creme caramel.
C Esquina s/n, Los Boliches, Fuengirola

El Tostón is a typical bodega, even if it is only seven years old. It's smoky, woody, with jamón legs hanging from the ceiling, and over 700 different types of wines available. People mostly perch on stools at small tables, enjoying the extensive modern tapas menu, while at the back there's a dining terrace for those who want to settle in for the evening. Tapas include chicory with roquefort sauce, or oyster mushrooms fried with garlic – a super balance of traditional and modern.
Edificio Terminal s/n, Fuengirola

Myramar Bar is lively and always busy. They have one of the most extensive selections of tapas in the area, as well as the bar dishes which are not on the menu. Tapas include pickles, hard cheeses, ensalada rusa, fish kebabs, prawn tortillas and croquettes.
C Jabega s/n

Granada tapas

Bodegas Castañedas is a traditional bodega that gets packed out with both locals and tourists. The lunchtime free tapa is generally a hot one – a stew or a rice dish, and there is a long list of other tapas and foods available: particularly popular are the raciones of local ham, and boards of cheeses and cured meats. There is a good wine list including some local wines, which are served, in classic bodega style, from the barrel.
C Almireceros 1

Casa Julio is a tiny bar, beautifully done out in blue and green tiles, tucked away down a narrow alleyway just off the Plaza Nueva. Fried slices of aubergine, anchovies, and marinaded dogfish are popular tapas. As for wines, try a glass of white from local wine-maker Horacio Calvente. In summer there are tables outside in the alley, and lots of customers. The service is always good.
C Hermosa 5

La Bodeguilla de al Lado is a little bar that not many people know about, not even the locals, but it's well worth seeking out. Fuensanta runs the bar on her own, dishing up good wines and gorgeous home-made tapas. These depend on the season: in spring she makes *tortilla de collejas*, a Spanish omelette made with spinach-like wild bladder campion (a traditional lenten dish); and in winter months you may be offered home-made paté with quince jelly or salt-cod. Her cheeses, cured sausages and home-cured olives are all delicious. The wine list contains examples from all over Spain, as well as reds from local bodegas such as Horacio Calvente and Señorío de Nevada. Closed 15 July to 15 September.
C Tendillas de Santa Paula s/n

Los Altramuces is located in a large square with a lively neighbourhood feel and lots of bars and restaurants. This is one of

the longest-established and most popular places to eat. Fernando Jiménez and his family opened the bar in 1946 on the other side of the square, and about eleven years ago moved to their current more spacious location. You can eat tapas and raciones inside at little tables, or in fine weather sit out on the busy terrace. Specialities of the house are pan-fried quail, deep-fried anchovies, lettuce hearts dressed with oil and vinegar, snails in sauce, and sautéed mushrooms with garlic. Most people order a selection of dishes to share: they are all delicious and very inexpensive.
Campo de Príncipe s/n

Los Diamantes is packed out almost as soon as the metal shutter rolls up. It may not be much to look at, inside or out, but by the time you've elbowed your way to the old-fashioned zinc counter of this *freiduría* (fried fish bar) you will realise why it is one of

Granada's favourite tapas spots. A free tapa comes with your drink: slices of crisp fried aubergine or a few tiny fried tentacles of squid, depending on what's frying that night. You can also order raciones, mostly of a range of fresh fish and seafood in light batter. Popular choices are anchovies and grilled prawns. Adventurous foodies should note that among the house specialities are fried sweetbreads and brain fritters.
C Navas 26

Málaga tapas
Antigua Casa de Guardia is an appropriate spot to try the local wine, as the place dates back to 1840 when Málaga wines were at the height of their popularity. The bar hasn't changed much over the last 165 years, with its huge barrels lining the walls. And it still serves traditional, local Málaga wines such as *pajarete* and *lágrima* straight from the cask. Waiters chalk up your total on the bar and you can buy seafood tapas from a refrigerated stand: there isn't a large selection – a few prawns and mussels and perhaps one or two other fishy bites – but what's on offer is really fresh. Picasso enjoyed the wines here, and on the wall there's a photograph of him being presented with a *jarra* by the bodega.
C Alameda Principal 18, Málaga

Bar Orellana is not much to look at from the outside, but nevertheless this is a very popular spot – and has been here for decades. Fans of its tapas spill out onto the street at busy times so get here early. Typical tapas include a stew of chickpeas, tripe, *morcilla* and *chorizo* served hot at lunchtime, and *bártolo*, a thin fillet of white fish, dipped in breadcrumbs and fried.
C Moreno Monroy 5

El Pimpi was once an old stable block and feed store. It has had the same owners for 32 years and it specialises in Andalucian wines, in particular fino and semi-sweet wines from Jerez, served with a range of tapas. Once you are through the unassuming entrance, the bar opens up into a beautiful terrace garden with extensive seating at the back and upstairs, with dozens of sherry barrels lining the walls. Frequented by actors, singers, writers and matadors, the ambience is low-key but buzzing with conversation.
C Granada 62

El Refectorium is one of the best places to eat in the city. It seethes with bullfighting fans, business folk and matadors on fight days, being located so close to the bullring. Tapas include seafood-stuffed peppers, lamb cooked in a saffron and tomato sauce, or mushrooms fried with serrano ham and lots of garlic.
C Cervantes 8

Marbella tapas

Cervecería Simón & El Abuelo Melquíades has a stand-up bar, a pavement terrace and a small restaurant, and has been serving great tapas to locals and visitors alike for the last 14 years. The menu is well translated, which is helpful for the uninitiated as there's bewildering array of choices, especially of fish dishes. Squid are always a good test of the chef's quality, and the ones here are tender and delicious. The *patatas bravas* are also very popular.
C Pablo Casals 1

El Strecho, which means "the narrow one", is a delightful place to kick off a tapas trail, and this bar – one of the best-known in the area – has thoughtfully put together a suggested route for you. Reasonable prices here, too, and a lively atmosphere.
C San Lázaro s/n

What to eat and where to find it

Foraging for food

Shopping in Andalucía

Out in the pueblos, the real trick is to spot a shop in the first place, because at first sight there often don't appear to be any. What you have to do is wander down that narrow street and keep an eye on every open door. Very often, there'll just be a nondescript fringe of plastic with no sign outside – but peer inside, and you'll find half the village there, engaged in their morning shop. Occasionally you'll come across a household selling their surplus produce: behind a slightly open door, there'll be a carefully positioned chair with a bowl of pristine white eggs or a basket of glossy chestnuts – genuine bounty, gently glowing in the shaft of light that finds it.

Food turns up for sale in other unlikely places, too. There may not be the roadside farm-stalls commonly found in other European countries, but you will often find bars with a corner devoted to the local chorizo, or that week's glut of courgettes.

Super markets

Markets are probably the best place to go shopping. In larger towns, there will be a municipal market that opens daily (except Sundays), although not all the stalls will be open every day – particularly on Mondays. Smaller villages are likely to have weekly markets. The best way to find these is simply to follow – at a discreet distance – those middle-aged ladies marching purposefully somewhere with an empty shopping trolley

trailing behind them. Of course, if your Spanish is good enough, you can always try asking …

It's not just that the produce for sale is fresher than at other shops, less packaged and so on; it's also an opportunity to take part in a local drama, with shoppers as the chorus, and stallholders as the stars of the show. Fishmongers in particular seem to have a real sense of the stage, hollering to their regular customers, and filleting fish with verve and a razor-edged knife. My own favourite markets are in Jerez and Sanlucár, as they fulfil my criteria of being busy, fun places to shop, with a cosy muddle of little shops and other stalls in the vicinity, and as an added bonus, they're attractive buildings too.

It has to be said, though, that this section could almost be called the good deli guide – because here in Andalucía you'll find that these shops are consistently excellent wherever you are: partly, this is a consequence of the huge range of charcuterie and excellent tinned food, all produced locally; but also it's because the shoppers are so discerning.

Supermarkets

At some stage you may have to do a basic shop, and inevitably these days that means a trip to the supermarket. There is a plethora of local, regional and national chains across Andalucía, but special mention should be made of the department store chain **El Corte Inglés**, which, besides stocking the usual clothing, cosmetics and electrics, also has superior food halls, and its own supermarket chain **Hipercor**. You'll normally find El Corte Inglés in city-central locations, and Hipercor on the outskirts: both have a *Club de Gourmets* section, carrying a terrific range of gourmet foods and wines from all over Spain. What's more, they also make an effort to feature local specialities. The Hipercor in Jerez, for example, is one of the few places that sells a large selection of top-notch sherries under one roof. Even better, El Corte Inglés will take orders over the internet or by phone, and deliver to you within 24 hours. Check out their website at www.elcorteingles.es.

A culinary tour of Seville

Any foodie visiting Andalucía should take time out to visit glamorous Seville. This city has everything, from flash restaurants, stylish cafés and workmen's bars, all serving brilliant food, to well-stocked delis on almost every corner. Take an extra suitcase when you go, because you'll be staggering back with a haul of gastronomic goodies that your kitchen simply cannot do without.

(1) **La Antigua** (C Pureza 12), located in the Triana district, is an outpost of Antigua Abacería de San Lorenzo (see 12 below) which is near the cathedral. It sells groceries, cheeses and charcuterie that customers are positively encouraged to try before buying. Flamenco music plays in the background, so you'll have to resist the urge to stamp your foot and shout *olé*, having downed a *fino* along with a chunk of delicious ewe's milk cheese from the Sierra Norte. This sierra is also the source of a lot of the game produce on sale, such as wild boar and venison. The tins of game patés include rabbit and partridge, and these are traditionally sold wrapped in greaseproof paper – a tradition that this shop has revived.

(2) **Mercado de Triana** is two minutes from La Antigua, right by the Isobel II bridge on Plaza del Altozano. This is a much jollier affair than the main market on C Pastor y Landero, which is rather gloomy and seems never to be very busy. At Triana, the permanent stalls are all gaily decorated with tiles declaring their specialities: tuna, snails, pigeon, partridge. There is also another 'temporary' market on the corner of C Regina and C Alcazares on Plaza de la Encarnación. It's been there temporarily since 1974, in fact, waiting for a nearby archaeological dig to finish, when work on a new market hall can start. In the meantime, it's a bustling lively place, with a great neighbourhood feel.

(3) **Semillas La Central** (C Regina 1) is a splendidly idiosyncratic combination of a hardware store, a gardening centre, and a spice emporium. The staff are a jolly bunch who are delighted that you are taking an interest in Andalucian cookery. Come here to buy pimentón by the scoopful. It is kept loose in glass-fronted drawers, with the picante version banished to another part of the shop so as not to adulterate the dulce (sweet) and the De La Vera pimentón.

(4) **Cuchillería Regina** (C Regina 4) is on the other side of the road from Semillas. This shop is heaven for any cook with a sharp knife fetish. It has every type of knife imaginable and some in shapes that you will never have come across before. Their chunky, almost semi-circular, *cuchillo filetero* looks like a medieval weapon. In fact you could even kit yourself out here as a sort of culinary knight, because they also sell steel mesh gloves that you are supposed to wear when carving ham – though strangely these turn out to be made in north Yorkshire. For a slightly different fancy-dress outfit, you could also buy your matador swords here. And fans of *jamón ibérico* take note: Señor Basalo, the owner, stocks those stands that you need when you have to grip a ham leg before slicing pieces off it. His Rolls-Royce version (which tilts and turns) is breathtakingly expensive and you'd have to be a restaurant owner or someone prepared to eat ham on a three-times-a-day basis to make it worth your while; but it is fun to take a look – if only to experience Señor Basalo's enthusiastic explanation of how it works. Incidentally, if you just happen

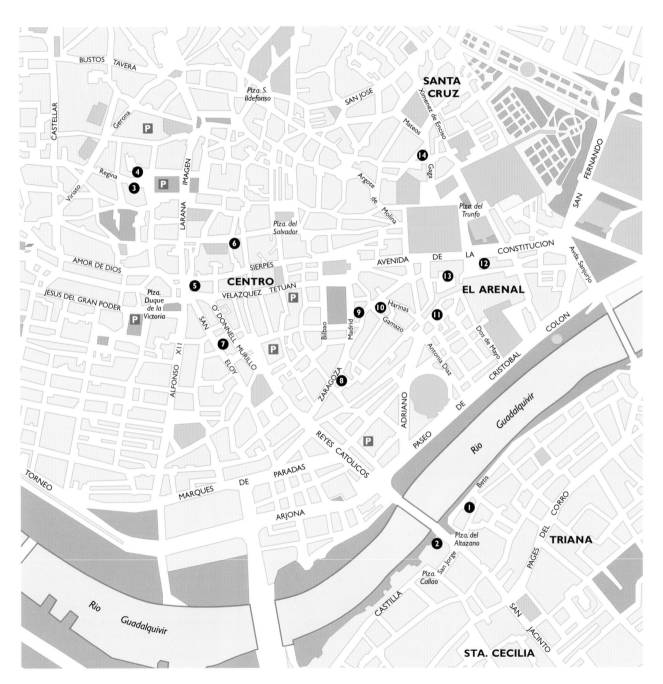

to be walking about Seville with a large knife that needs sharpening, well, he will happily hone it for you.

(5) **La Campana** (C Sierpes 1) is one of the top *pastelerías* in the city. There's a zinc bar at one end where people crowd round for a coffee, and fabulous friezes of cherubs on the walls. The muffins are a world away from the mass-produced apologies so commonly available elsewhere. These are glistening with pomegranate seeds, and crusty with lava flows of chocolate. Besides the elaborate cakes, you may also be tempted by the big slabs of chocolate – there's even a handy mallet to smash them up into more manageable pieces.

(6) **Baco** (C Cuna 4) is a local chain of delis, and this branch is probably the biggest of the ones in central Seville. The shop is a mix of everyday and exotic groceries, pungent cheeses and hard-to-come-by sherries. One of the features here is the extensive range of salt-cod or *bacalao*: there are even vacuum packs of the pre-desalinated stuff. So now you have no excuse not to try one of our bacalao recipes.

(7) **San Eloy** (C San Eloy 31) is halfway down the street on the left-hand side. If anyone has ever pondered whether it is possible to have a discount deli, here is your answer. Salt-cod is scattered randomly on the counter; hams hang in higgledy-piggledy fashion; and the floor looks like it could do with a good scrub. But prices are certainly lower than in the other delis, though your Spanish will need to be pretty fair to deal with the busy staff. The owners also have a tapas bar round the corner.

(8) **Vinotempo** (C Zaragoza 64) is a rather classy wine merchant's, selling a good range from the lesser-known bodegas of Spain. They have a wine club too, which is free to join, and once you are a member you are invited to tasting events and entitled to discounts on cases. And yes, they will ship to countries outside Spain. Find out more on 954 210 659.

(9) **Heladería La Florentina** (C Zaragoza 16) has a lovely range of ice creams to revive weary feet and flagging spirits. Seville can be incredibly hot – at least that is the excuse you can give yourself, as you try and decide between the chocolate, or the cinnamon, or the cheesecake, or perhaps even the Seville cream ... This could just turn out to be a shop to which you find yourself making a daily detour.

meaning a small grocery shop, and this one is another on the Casa Moreno model, combining a store with a bar where you can eat. Owner Vicente Delgado wants customers to round off their shopping with a sip of sherry, a couple of tapas and a chat. Of course, the tapas are made from the products available in the shop. And the beauty of this is obvious: before you buy an unfamiliar piece of fresh meat, for example, perhaps veal cheek or venison, you can nibble a cooked bit first. There is no kitchen on the premises, though, so the tapas are either those that require no cooking, or ones that have been made in Vicente's own kitchen at home. Try to visit here on Friday lunchtimes, because that is when this home cooking is on the menu.

(13) **El Torno** (Plaza del Cabildo s/n) is the place to come to if you don't have time to visit the convents (see page 50 if you do). This little shop is hidden behind wooden latticed shutters in a suitably monastic manner, and sells cookies, cakes, honey and jams from most of the cloistered orders in the area. The *tortas de hoja*, made by the convent of San Andrés, are especially delicious: they're similar to *tortas de aceite* in shape – and they're wrapped in greaseproof paper too – but the pastry is more flaky.

(14) **La Delicia del Barrio** (C Mateos Gago 15) specialises in olive oil from all over Andalucía. There's a marvellous range, not just of brands but also of container sizes, from dinky bottles to two-litre cans. This shop stocks everything: olive mill stones; El Callejón, the oil made from the original variety of wild olive called *acebuche* in Spanish; and excellent big brand names, like *1881* produced in Osuna.

(10) **Casa Moreno** (C Gamazo 7) is one of the few remaining original examples of the store-cum-bar that used to be so common in Seville. It's a wonderful combination: you take your pick of ham, cheese or whatever takes your fancy from the store at the front, and then wander through to the memorabilia-laden bar at the back. It's small, smoky, and jolly – with a bull's head looming over the zinc counter, and masses of signed photos of matadors on the walls adding to the atmosphere. The shelves reach up to the rafters, laden with tinned goods such as smoked cod's liver, cockles, and green peppers stuffed with mushrooms or prawns. At ground level, fifteen or so varieties of pulses are displayed in sacks. The charcuterie is all local – for example, the cured pork loin is from Jerez; while the tuna roe, salted anchovies and *mojama* are sourced in Barbate.

(11) **El Reloj** (C Arfe 18) has a wonderfully traditional decor that hasn't changed since 1894. Francisco and Antonio Ruiz Gordillo, the owners, pride themselves on sourcing the best quality products, several of which come from Huelva province: the chickpeas come from Aracena; the El Lazo *ibérico* ham is from Cortegana; Molino de San Nicolás y San Esteban olive oil (which recently won a gold medal in America, see page 53) is produced in Beas; and the very special Columel vinegar comes from La Palma del Condado.

(12) **Antigua Abacería de San Lorenzo** (C Almirantazgo 8) is located very close to the *Postigo del Aceite*, the Oil Gate, which is one of Seville's last remaining city gates. It acquired the name because olive growers had to pay a toll before they could enter the city with their oil. *Abacería* is a word derived from Arabic,

A culinary tour of Granada

Granada has an eclectic mix of traditional and trendy shops concentrated in the streets below and around the cathedral: shops selling more kinds of knives than you could ever have imagined existed, along with up-to-the-minute fashions, fans and lace, baskets, local pottery, kitchen equipment (at the very good and large ferretería on the Plaza Bib-Rambla), flouncy, spotty, colourful flamenco dresses ... and some wonderful food shops.

The heart of food shopping in the city centre is really the Mercado de San Agustín, the central market. But it has to be said that, despite its good quality foodstuffs, it's a rather severe-looking modern building, and you may find that it's more fun to do what lots of other people prefer to do: shop in the open air at the stalls that spill out onto the nearby squares.

(1) A good starting point is with the many spice and herb sellers who set up their tables on C Cárcel Baja. Here you will find not only numerous aromatic and colourful herbs and spices for cooking, but medicinal ones too. They've all got helpful labels listing the treatments they are supposed to provide, from curing a cold to making you slim.

There are several other open-air fruit and veg markets scattered throughout the city, where smallholders and peasant farmers come to sell their wares, including C San Agustín, Plaza Pescadería and Plaza de la Romanilla. The latter is especially worth a visit: old men selling bunches of herbs and tiny black dried olives, as well as gypsies selling snails they have collected from the countryside in large buckets.

(2) **La Alacena** (C San Jerónimo 3) is located in one of the best shopping streets, with an authentic neighbourhood feel. The shop is run by James Carter and his wife, Rosa Moreno Rodríguez, who eight years ago decided to set up in business because "there was no shop like this in Granada." La Alacena stocks typically Andalucian products like sherry wines and vinegars, but the duo really specialise in sourcing food and wine from the province of Granada. Their honey comes from Órgiva in the Alpujarras, as do the goat's milk cheeses, while the *jamón serrano* is particularly delicious and special: James has managed to find a ham producer who feeds his pigs on a diet of olives. As for olive oils, check out Alomartes from Granada, and Basilipo from Carmona in Seville province. The latter is made from *arbequina* olives which are more commonly found in Catalonia.

Don't forget to try *queso de almendra* – which is not a cheese as the name suggests,

Pl. Santa
Ana

Gomérez

de

Cuesta

Plaza
Nueva

Almireceros

❼

Gran   Vía   de   Colón

Plaza de
Isabel
la Católica

Pl.
Descalzas

Pavaneras

Sta.

Jesús y María

Pl. Santo
Domingo

**SAN
MATÍAS**

Varela

❶

❷

Baja

CATEDRAL

Reyes

Católicos

San

Jerónimo

Pie de la Torre

San

Matías

❻

Cuesta del Progreso

❺

Pl.
Romanilla

Colegio

Catalino

Plaza
Bib-
Rambla

Ganivet

❹   **❸**

Lucena

Pescadería

Salamanca

Ángel

Carrera
del Genil

Puerta
Real de
España

Acera   del   Darro

Tablas

Calle de San   Antón

Calle

Calle

Puentezuelas

Recogidas

**SAN
ANTÓN**

Verónica   de   la   Magdalena

but a confection that has a hard outer layer of white chocolate, and a type of marzipan inside made from ground almonds, sugar, lemon, and egg white. It's an ancient recipe, dating from Moorish times, and is still made in the Granadine village of Murtas.

La Alacena has wines from all over Spain including a good selection – as you'd expect – from Andalucía. Apart from wines from Jerez, Montilla-Moriles and Málaga, they also have some red wines from up-and-coming wine bodegas in Granada like Horacio Calvente and Señorío de Nevada, as well as an organic red Barranco Oscuro.

La Alacena also despatches goods by post to the UK, and there is now a wine-selling branch of the business operating from the UK.

(3) **Ora et Labora** (Plaza Pescadería 7) means 'prayer and work', and this shop is run by two sisters (a third sister is a nun who, naturally, makes *dulces de convento*) who stock products from convents and monasteries from all over Spain. There's a big range of biscuits, meringues, cookies, and sweets; also angel's-hair jam, and quince jelly; and of course liqueurs. Visit at Christmas and Easter time and you'll also find other goodies such as yemas, which are candied egg yolks.

(4) **Comestibles Cristóbal** (Plaza Pescadería 13) specialises in excellent local hams, black puddings, chorizos, and other cured and uncured pork products – many from the Granadine village of Zujaira. They also sell ham bones for making stocks and soups, as well as salt-cod, and a variety of tinned goods.

(5) **La Casa de las Matanzas** (Plaza de la Romanilla 11) literally means 'the pig killing shop'. At first sight it all seems normal enough: peeled almonds, pine nuts, dried peppers, dried chillis, salt-cod, coffees and teas, dried pulses, spices and herbs. They also sell their own freshly ground mix of spices and seasonings for *pinchos morunos*, the Moorish kebabs that are so popular in Andalucía. But venture to the back of the shop and you'll notice a plastic bin with a lid, which only strong-stomached and seriously-committed carnivores should investigate. For inside are skeins and skeins of pigs' intestines, which sausage fanatics use to make their home-made chorizos and black puddings. The annual *matanza* (the killing and butchering of a pig) in rural villages is not as common as it was, but the older generation – and other gourmands – still want to make their own sausages, and so they come here for the proper ingredients.

(6) **La Oliva** (C Rosario 9) is a treasure trove of gourmet foods. Francisco Lillo is a

champion of artisan producers, and he sources "jewels", as he likes to call them, from the ancient kingdom of Granada, which in modern-day geography would be the provinces of Granada, Málaga and Almería.

Francisco encourages customers to try before they buy: "I like people to make their own discoveries about what they like. *Jamón ibérico* is all the rage at the moment because people think it's the best cured ham there is. But there are many people who, when they come to try it, are surprised to find that they prefer a good *jamón serrano*." Mind you, don't neglect to try his *ibérico* ham – which doesn't come from Jabugo, but from a village in Granada called Bracana.

Other "jewels" include a gorgeous goat's cheese called Blanca Serrana. It's produced in Archidona, in Málaga province, using the milk from an almost extinct breed of goat. The jams are made by the Comendadores de Santiago nuns, and, alongside the usual fruit ones such as orange or cherry, there is also a jam the nuns call sweet potato cream. These are packaged in attractive earthenware pots and make great presents.

He stocks some unusual spirits and liqueurs too. Espino Negro, for example, is an excellent *pacharán*, a kind of sloe gin, made in Monachil in the Sierra Nevada from locally-grown sloes. Montero rum from Motril is hard to come by, but you can buy it here. As for wines, Francisco is particularly proud of his Marenas red, made by José Márquez Herrador in Montilla.

(7) Mantequería Castellano
(C Almicereros 6) is a family business specialising in hams. The present owner's grandfather had the job of selecting and seasoning meat at a local award-winning charcuterie factory. This was an important job since in those days adding salt, pepper and wine to sausages was always done by hand. Manuel Castellano continues this honourable tradition. He sells *reserva* hams, mostly from white pigs, which are hung for 18 months; *gran reserva* hams hang for 24 months or longer.

Manuel makes an unusual *queso de cerdo*, literally "pork cheese", which is similar to old-fashioned English brawn. It is made by cooking pigs' heads in lard and white wine. When the meat is soft, it's chopped, fried and seasoned with pepper, nutmeg and white wine, and then pressed and left for a day.

He also sells non-porky things like a fig jam, which won an award in 2004 as one of the top ten products from Andalucía, and local wines from La Sierra de Contraviesa and Baza.

Granada outskirts

Alfacar
About four minutes' drive from the city of Granada is Alfacar, "the village of bread". The tradition of bread-making in Alfacar goes back to the times of the Moors. In the seventeenth century the village had five bread ovens and six flour mills: now it has an incredible eighty or so bakeries, producing breads of all kinds; and many use traditional wood-fired ovens. The bakers of the village claim that some of their bread-making success is due to the good local spring water. One very popular loaf is the crusty and slightly chewy *pan rústico* or *pan de pueblo* – country-style bread. You can buy bread directly from the bakeries: they start work at about 2am and sell bread up until midday.

Baked potato seller in Granada

Alcudia

About eight kilometres from Guadix, which is famous for its hundreds of inhabited cave dwellings, you will find the village of Alcudia, at one time a Moorish village. Here you can buy the most delicious loaves baked in wood-fired ovens: they come in several sizes, the largest being a round, three-kilo loaf, which is said to keep for two to three days. And if you should fancy something to accompany your loaf, pop into one of the several *carnicerías*, or butcher's shops, because Alcudia's other claim to fame is its excellent *charcutería*, and particularly its black puddings and chorizos.

Shopping around: Córdoba, Málaga, Cádiz and Jaén

Córdoba

At first glance, Córdoba doesn't look like an object of culinary pilgrimage, despite (or perhaps because of) the millions of tourists who flock here. There are, however, several places worth tracking down, particularly if you've got a sweet tooth.

Alimentación Andalusí (C Rodríguez Marín 22), just north of Plaza de la Corredera, is a delightful deli that serves the local neighbourhood rather than passing tourists. Its shelves reach right up into the rafters, loaded with precariously balanced tinned game and fish; nearer the ground, large baskets of dried pulses and beans jostle with cartons of dried cod; at the counter, salamis and hams are cut to order by two very jolly assistants.

On the south side of the Plaza is a market, consisting of a row of small fruit and veg stalls, and a much larger fish and meat hall to the rear. If you lived in the area you'd no doubt shop here, but it probably isn't worth a special trip – not least because of the nightmare of parking.

Bodegas Mezquita (Corregidor Luis de la Cerda 73) faces the mosque complex, and probably half its visitors are tourists who are lost – but who linger on to discover a treasure trove of produce from the province of Córdoba. Here there is an excellent range of Montilla-Moriles wines. Owner Baldomero Gas is particularly enthusiastic about Segunda Bota, a fino by Bodegas Delgado in Puerto Genil. This is aged for eight years in the solera system and has won a Baco award.

Córdoban olive oils are well-known in Spain; here they stock nine or ten different varieties from Doña Mencia, Cabra, and Nuñez de Prado from Baena (see page 53 for more details). The shop holds olive oil tasting sessions to help people get to know what the terms peppery, fruity, strong and mild really mean in terms of taste. They also sell extra virgin olive oil soaps: each type has a different use – for children, for moisturising, as an antiseptic, and so on.

The shop stocks a range of soups and jams made by a women's co-operative called La Despensa, based in Villarubia. The honey is from Montoro, the cured hams and pork are produced in the Valle de los Pedroches, the cheeses in olive oil are from the sierras, and the *membrillo* is from Puerto Genil. There are some pretty unusual liqueurs too: how about prickly pear? All the products are hand-made, using traditional methods; quite a few are organic as well. Big spenders take note: the shop offers free local delivery if you buy more than €30 worth of goodies. For more information, there's a website, www.bodegasmezquita.com

Roldán (C Dr Marañon 9) is part of a Córdoban chain of cake and chocolate shops – well worth a visit, although perhaps the easiest branch to locate is on the railway station concourse. Somehow time just seems to melt away when you tuck into their moist, not-quite-sticky almond sponge with a rubble of caramel coated walnuts heaped on top. Their chocolate cake is equally heavenly, but the house speciality is *regaña*, a savoury pastry that originates from the Guadalquivir valley.

Once upon a time sailors used to take on board with them a sort of bread, made with olive oil and flavoured with sesame seeds, that kept for months (well, weeks anyhow), and along the way, some canny baker started making this bread commercially; nowadays Roldán make it in stick form and has a factory dedicated to its production just to keep up with demand.

Other delights include a cake called Zaira (the name of a princess from the Córdoban palace of Medina Azahara) which sounds straight out of the Arabian Nights, and it's no surprise to find that it's a sponge with cream and walnuts and a layer of caramelised egg cream, topped off with flambéed meringue and decorated with fruit. Ideal for any wannabe princess's birthday, whether she's eight, eighteen or eighty-eight. And don't forget to try the ice creams: one of their inventions is curd cheese with *tocino de cielo*, a kind of creme caramel. For more information, their website can be found at www.pasteleriaroldan.com

Confitería Serrano (C Concepción 3) is one of five in this chain of cake shops. They pride themselves on only using real cream and extra virgin olive oil – nothing synthetic, and no substitutes for the real thing. All their cakes are hand-made – "the largest machine

we have is the oven," remarked the owner, Bernardo Serrano. House specialities include a Córdoban delicacy made with crystallised pumpkin jelly and cinnamon flavoured pastry. www.confiteriaserrano.com

Despensa Serrano (Plaza Ramón y Cajal 1) belongs to the same family as the Serrano pastry shops, and it's a two-level enterprise with local deli products on one floor, and a big selection of wines on the other. Of particular interest are the wine-tasting sessions and the courses run by their in-house oenologist. If you're interested in different vintages from one area, or in what Spain has to offer in terms of *cava* sparkling wines, then Serrano can organise a specialist course just for you. Telephone 957 474 739 for more details.

Málaga

For millions of people, Málaga was for many years no more than an airport. Now it's on the tourist map because of the newly opened Picasso museum, in honour of its most famous son (not including Antonio Banderas, that is). And the city also has some good food shopping around the centre. Start at the end of Málaga's main shopping street, Calle Márques de Larios.

Charcutería Central (C María) is a delicatessen attached to a café – which wouldn't raise an eyebrow in Britain perhaps, but it's unusual in this part of the world. The café in question is the buzzing but traditional-style Café Central, which has a terrace overlooking the square that's ideal for people-watching. You can enter through the café itself, on Plaza de la Constitución, or through a door directly into the shop on Calle María, just round the corner. The shop has an old-fashioned grocery feel about it, and, even better, has knowledgeable and enthusiastic

La Mallorquina (Plaza Felix Sáenz s/n) is very popular. You may have to wait a little while to be served, but that allows you time to take in the wide range of foods in this well-stocked deli. It has all the usual cheeses, hams and other pork products but also stocks some more old-fashioned delicacies like *callos* (tripe, ready to eat), *mojama* (dried tuna), and three types of *morcilla* (black pudding). This is a good place to stock up your store-cupboard with locally-produced *caña de miel*, molasses made from sugar cane grown on the coast, quince jelly, and tins and jars of gourmet vegetables.

Cádiz

The city of Cádiz is thought to be the oldest city in Europe, being founded as Gadir by the Phoenicians in about 1100 BC. It has always been a great centre for trading wine, olive oil and all manner of preserved fish throughout its chequered history. The coastal towns between Cádiz and Tarifa were big producers of *garum* for the Romans (this is a condiment, rather similar to the Thai fish sauce *nam pla*); and they continue now to be the centre for the production of *mojama*, salt-cured tuna.

Cádiz is built on a long thin promontory and is very nearly an island, so it is scarcely surprising that fish and seafood are the most typical products to be found locally. In fact, the fried fish in Cádiz is some of the best you'll come across in Andalucía, with plenty of *freidurías* around the city where you can buy fried fish to take away, including *boquerones* (anchovies), *cazón en adobo* (marinaded dogfish), *pijotas* (small whiting), *choco frito* (fried cuttlefish), and *acedias* (small sole). One of the best is Freiduría Las Flores in Plaza de las Flores.

In terms of food shops, two certainly rate a mention:

staff behind the counter. It stocks a good range of hams, chorizos, black puddings, and cured sausages from two main areas: Guijuelo in Salamanca, and, more locally, Ronda. You can also buy specialist tinned foods, cheeses, quince jelly, Málaga raisins, dried figs and other foods produced nearby.

Zoilo (C Granada 65), opposite the Church of Santiago where Picasso was baptised, is a tiny delicatessen packed with interesting goodies, and run by the same family for the last fifty years or so. It has tinned, dried and bottled goods, cheeses, and pork products from all over Spain. Of particular interest are the marinaded anchovies, pickled capers, Mallorcan *sobrasada*, goat's cheese from Ronda, and *cecina*, which is dried beef.

La Dehesa (Alameda Principal 11) is a small bar and shop which specialises in hams (both *serrano* and *ibérico*), chorizos, cured

sausages and other pork products from the locality and from other parts of Spain. Try them with a drink, and then buy.

Mercado Central de Atarazanas (C Atarazanas 8) is built on the site of what was once a Moorish boatyard. The main entrance is the old gateway to the yard, and dates from the fourteenth century: the rest of the market was built in neo-Mudejar style in the nineteenth century. The building is long overdue for renovation but is all the more fun for it: it has a great atmosphere and it's a fab place to go shopping. Good stalls (among many) to look out for are: Armando Cuberos, a *charcutería* (between stands 21 and 22) which has good chorizo from Ronda, along with cheeses from the Alpujarras region of Granada, and black pudding from Jabugo; also stand number 16 which has lots of lovely spices and seasonings.

La Alacena de Cádiz (C Santo Tomás 2) is an excellent establishment that sells wine and gastronomic specialities from Cádiz province, including olive oil, cheese, fish preserves and charcuterie. The owner is very knowledgeable and well worth seeking out.

Miña Tierra (C Cristóbal Colón 7-9) is stuffed to the gills with a great selection of wines, cheeses, charcuterie, and tinned and bottled products.

Jaén

The province of Jaén is one of the olive oil-producing epicentres of the planet – a fact you'll find easy to believe if you decide to visit the area. After driving for hours from the costas through uninterrupted olive tree orchards, you look up at what appears to be the outskirts of a nondescript agricultural town tumbled across a hill-top, and you wonder if the effort is going to be worth it.

Baeza

It is. Baeza is a charming, huggable-sized world heritage city, and as a consequence it's very popular with weekending Spanish. Which is good news for other intrepid gourmands, because there are at least a dozen good restaurants in town to cater for this regular, demanding clientele.

In terms of shopping, you'll be spoilt for choice when it comes to sweet pastries since just about every other shop seems to be a café or *pastelería*. **Morral** (Portales Tundidores 14) overlooks the main square, Plaza de la Constitución, and the townsfolk consider it to be the best. It's been going since 1866, although the shop is a basic marble-tiled, neon-lit affair rather than a baroquely decorated café. The speciality is a type of *hojaldres*, a flaky pastry filled with angel's-hair pumpkin jam and covered in icing

Baeza

sugar, called *pastel baezano*. Those who don't have such a sweet tooth should try their *almendrados de Baeza*, florentine-shaped sweets made with chopped toasted almonds and plain chocolate.

At the entrance to the Plaza is **La Casa del Aceite** (Paseo de la Constitución 9), where you can buy catering-sized jars of green olives, and choose from a huge range of local olive oils. They also stock pastries, lots of them, including muffins or *magdalenas* from the Monasterio de San Antonio, located on the other side of town. Alongside all the food, they also stock olive oil soap and shampoo, olive wood knick-knacks, and local pottery.

You can visit several of the olive oil haciendas too. **La Laguna**, 9 km south of Baeza, is a special example, in terms not just of its wonderful location, but also of what

you can do here. If you want to stock up on oil, you can visit the refinery and sample some before buying. Then if you pootle down the estate drive you can visit the immaculately restored olive oil museum. This has different olive varieties growing in the courtyard, and the various methods of oil extraction housed and explained indoors.

The museum is located next to a catering college or *escuela de hostelería*. The college is part of a government initiative, and there are now four of them in Andalucía: the others are in Málaga, Cádiz and Huelva. What makes them so special is that the students are practising on paying customers. Their informal restaurant, called La Campana, serves straightforward, traditional Jaén cooking. If you are an out-of-season visitor, though, you should note that during the winter months it is open only at the weekends.

The second restaurant at the complex, La Capilla, is open throughout the year and concentrates on more elaborate food. Dishes include monkfish with a red pepper sauce served with sweetbreads; or venison, chestnut and pomegranate ragout. Puddings are gorgeous: try the olive oil ice cream and the sticky chocolate brownies with peach foam. The waiters can look a little anxious when they have to practise their English language and their serving skills both at once, but it all adds to the charm of the place. Last but not least, there's even a small bird reserve, Laguna Grande, where you can walk off lunch.

Hacienda La Laguna, Puente del Obispo, Jaén Tel (for restaurants): 953 771 005 Web: www.ehlaguna.com

Úbeda

Baeza's twin, Úbeda, is another, slightly larger, world heritage city, on a neighbouring

hilltop. As at Baeza, the abundance of Renaissance architecture generates a feeling of genteel good taste and wealth.

Los Candiles (C Rastro 23) is the best deli in town. The counter is barely visible, thanks to the stacks of cookies and breads, which are all made by the local convent. Try the *ochios* – they're savoury rusks made with olive oil and paprika and are a welcome change from more usual sugar-drenched biscuits.

There are fifteen different types of Spanish cheese to choose from, and a good selection of chorizos and other sausages from nearby Cazorla. Olive oils are piled high like breakfast cereals in a supermarket: the main brands on offer are Oro Magina from the Sierra Magina, and Unioliva, one of the local co-operatives. The wine section includes bottles from the Alpujurras.

Palacios (Corredera San Fernando 4) is a rococo-decorated *confitura* and café. Work your way past the cupids to the back of the shop if you want to sit down for a *con leche*. The coffee served here is one of the better cups you'll come across; you can either go local and have it with toast dripping in olive oil, or you can just opt for a croissant.

If you are someone who loves the combination of chocolate and nuts, then this shop is your bonbon heaven. There's white chocolate with walnuts, hazelnuts with plain, and just about every variation in between. There is also a selection of estate-grown chocolate.

Rincón del Jamón (Corredera San Fernando 18) is a *charcutería* featuring an outstanding selection of dry-cured hams, with legs from Guadix and Jabugo lining the walls. The shop assistants are happy to let you sample slivers before making a decision.

The municipal market is at the end of San Fernando and it's interesting see how different it is from those on the other side of the region, like Jerez. Here in Úbeda there are many more meat stalls, and the quality and range of fish isn't quite as staggeringly good. Check out the egg stall, though – it's heaped high, with not a sign of an egg box anywhere: bring your own, if you don't want a *revuelto* in your car boot.

Finally, if you haven't yet had your fill of olive oil, head for the **Museo de la Oliva** (C Gradas 13). It is open seven days a week and features an education section on how oil is extracted and why it's so good for you, along with a comprehensive selection of oils from the area, along with T-shirts and mugs.

Shopping in the sierras

Never very far away from the costas, another Andalucía shimmers on the horizon: the milk-washed, bruised blues of the multiple sierras. It's a countryside that, on closer inspection, turns out to be the burnt-out bleached browns and blondes of a surfer's hair, while the heat turns the sky a breathless grey.

In other words, it's distinctly tricky trying to take decent photographs. So abandon the camera, and arm yourself with a large basket and plenty of curiosity before heading for the hills.

Sierra de Aracena: Jabugo

This remote little town owes its living to *jamón ibérico* and is one of the places to make a pilgrimage, if you have a passion for ham, for it's home to top producers **Sánchez Romero Carvajal** (Ctra San Juan del Puerto s/n; tel: 959 121 194). This is not some anonymous concrete-clad factory, but an old-fashioned bodega with its very own tapas bar and shop attached. And it is certainly the place to come if you want to buy a whole leg of *jamón*.

They will do guided tours, if there is a group of you, and what you'll see depends upon the time of year. Autumn and winter is when the fresh hams are buried in sea salt: for every kilo in weight, a ham spends a whole day dehydrating. After this, it's washed and put into humidity-controlled chambers to let the salt penetrate the muscle. The hams are then hung from the bodega ceilings to dry: three months for every kilo. It's an extraordinary sight and smell – not unpleasant, mind you – to walk through millions of hams, gently growing a flor (*penicillium roqueforti*, the same fungus that's used in making the cheese) and developing

its flavour. It must be especially good fun if you're a major consumer of ham, like a restaurant or a shop, because you can come along and pick the legs you want, even before they are ready.

Meanwhile, in the barely-lit, smoke-laden drying rooms upstairs, there's a distinctly gothic, gates of Hell atmosphere, with Holm oak log fires smouldering on the floor and thousands of sausages hanging from the ceilings.

Sánchez Romero Carvajal's top brand is 5J – *Cinco Jotas* – and this name has entered the Spanish language as an expression analogous to 'top drawer' or 'the bee's knees'.

Los Pueblos Blancos

The White Towns is the collective name for the stardust scattering of towns and villages that stretch from Arcos de la Frontera in Cádiz Province to Ronda in the province of Málaga. As well as all those precariously balanced, beautiful whitewashed buildings for you to admire, they have a lot to offer on the gastronomic front.

The area is well-known in Andalucía for its vegetables – in particular artichokes, wild asparagus and chard – as well as two types of edible thistle, from which the fleshy part of the young leaves is used. So look out for local dishes such as *tortilla de trigueros* (wild asparagus omelette), *acelgas con patatas* (chard with potatoes), *garbanzos con esparragos trigueros* (chickpeas with wild asparagus), and *berza de cardillo y tagarninas* (thistle stew).

Carnivores are well catered for too. The lamb can be wonderful, especially in the more mountainous regions. If you see leg of young lamb on the menu in places like Zahara de la Sierra or Grazalema, then go for it – it'll be excellent. Another popular dish is *caldereta de cordero*, lamb stew. Dishes made using game are also very common, especially rabbit, partridge, venison and wild boar.

As for shops and markets, check out these:

Antequera
Mercado de Abastos
Most towns and villages have a permanent market, and some are better than others. Mercado de Abastos in Antequera is well worth a visit, as it has some great local produce. For a start, it has a specialist organic stand, La Ecohuerta at number 22, with all kinds of goodies including preserves, honeys, olives, olive oils and vinegars. Meanwhile, María del Carmen Rodríguez, guardian of stall number 37, stocks seasonal fruit, herbs and vegetables, some of which have been grown in the family's veggie garden. Of particular note are her own home-dried peppers. What's more, she'll happily give you recipes and tips – in Spanish, mind – to encourage you with some of her less familiar produce.
Plaza de Abastos, Antequera

Arcos de la Frontera
El Descansillo
This is just a really sweet deli. The owner, Rocío Giselle Ampuero Abad, stocks a variety of local produce: a pungent, hard goat's cheese; an olive oil produced from the original variety of olive, *sylvestre*, that has a lovely soft, fat taste; and the town's favourite bread, which looks like an Italian focaccia but is sweet and flavoured with fennel seed; also a wide selection of wines. Even better, she opens the shop on a Sunday, so if you fancy a last-minute picnic, this is the place to come and buy the makings.
C Cuesta de Belén 6, Arcos de la Frontera
Web: www.eldescansilloarcos.com

Rancho Cortesano
Museo de la Miel y las Abejas
Down the road from Arcos, about 10 minutes' drive outside of Jerez, is this honey and bees museum; actually it's more of an educational farm shop geared towards the little ones. Be warned, though, that your children (and you) will need to speak a little Spanish to understand some of the exhibits, although no language is really necessary just to enjoy watching the bees in their hives – all firmly behind glass. The shop counter has a tasting tray for their honey range, which includes eucalyptus, rosemary, oak, orange and mountain flowers. The latter is for sale in 5kg plastic containers, as well as the more usual 400g jars. Pollen, royal jelly, pottery jars and a delicious-smelling home-made lavender and honey soap are also for sale. Outside, there is a playground and picnic area with views across the farmland. If this is too far out of your way, though, you'll find that the deli in Arcos also stocks their honeys.
Ctra Cortés-Cuartillo km 2; in the direction of El Torno
Tel: 956 237 528
Web: www.ranchocortesano.com

Benalauría
La Molienda Verde
Benalauría isn't quite as touristy as some of the other white villages, and is all the prettier for it. Foodies with a green tinge to their consciences should make tracks here if only to visit La Molienda Verde, which is an offshoot of the now well-known and busy Mesón La Molienda (see page 17). The shop is run as a co-operative and sells local produce prepared in as environmentally friendly a way as possible. Non-organic products include fruit compotes, preserves and fruits in brandy. The organic range includes preserved green asparagus, dried

Ronda

tomatoes and peppers, aubergines in chestnut sauce, and whatever vegetables are in season.

C Cruz 33, Benalauría

Benaoján
Icarben

Twenty or so minutes' drive from Ronda is the village of Benaoján. Most people come this way to visit the nearby Cueva de la Pileta with its famous prehistoric cave paintings. However, another reason is Icarben, a small factory producing all kinds of pork products: the range has over sixty different tasty and traditional combinations of bits of pig. There are cured hams, both *serrano* and *ibérico*, along with salamis, chorizos, black puddings, and cured and uncured sausages. You can also buy patés, *sobrasada*, *zurrapa* (which is a lard seasoned with spices and pork pieces), and ham bones for making soups and stocks.

Zone de la Vega s/n, Benaoján

Ronda
Jamonería Berrocal

This is located on Calle Espinel, the main pedestrianised shopping street that starts at the bullring and is known locally as Calle la Bola. The shop stocks cured hams, sausages, chorizos and black pudding, all sourced locally from the nearby mountains, the Serranía de Ronda. How much you buy is up to you – whether it's a whole ham, a large chunk or just a few slices. They also stock wines and local goat's and ewe's milk cheeses.

C Espinel 112, Ronda

Sierra de Cazorla: Cazorla

Heaven knows what happens when it snows in this village. The gradients along the narrow twisty lanes are perfectly lethal, even when the weather is dry and warm. The trouble is, it's impossible not to let your gaze stray up to that stunning mountain scenery, when you really should be keeping a watchful eye on those tricky pavements. Keen walkers will love this area, though, and there's plenty of excellent food to revive them here after a day's clamber. **Embutidos Carrasco** (C Dr Muñoz 15) is a well-stocked deli with a good bread section tucked away behind all the chorizos and sausages. If you want a really memorable shopping experience, then head for **Manolo's** (Plaza Santa María s/n). You'll recognise it by the "quad bike for hire" sign outside, but don't let this put you off. Inside is an extraordinary den of eclectic produce: cowmen's leather hats and deer-fur satchels vying for business with rafters laden down with hams from the Alpujarras and baskets heaped with deer and wild boar chorizos, all locally-made. In the chill cabinet you'll find Cazorla goat's cheeses, one of which is a hard-textured nutty-tasting delicacy with an extra tang provided by its

rosemary-covered rind. It doesn't have a name, apparently, so just point it out and ask for a taste. There's also excellent *morcilla blanca*, made with pork meat, eggs, saffron and masses of garlic. Cazorla has its own *Denominación de Origen* extra virgin olive oil, and here you'll find bottles of the exclusive *royal* olive variety as well as the more common *picual*. Manolo is enthusiastic about everything he has for sale, and he speaks a bit of English too. You could well find yourself leaving not only with enough food to feed ten stout hikers, but also with an unfeasibly large hay-fork made from a single pine tree trunk – something you hadn't previously realised you wanted to own.

Sierra Nevada

High altitude Trevelez is an ideal location for drying hams. The factory here is modern and a bit disappointing to visit if you are expecting the romance of an old bodega, but there are plenty of ham shops in the village. One example is the excellent **Jamonería Al-Andalus** (C El Puente, s/n), which has a branch down in Motril called **Mesón La Despensa** (Av Salobreña 8) if you don't feel like the trek to the mountains. Besides Trevelez ham, this attractive blue-tiled shop is stuffed full of goodies like hand-made chocolate from Granada, and wines and cheeses from the Alpujarras.

Meanwhile in Dúrcal, the family-run business of **Jamones Ríos** (C Pablo Picasso 2) still continues the traditional methods of hand-curing and drying hams, producing over 5,000 of them a year.

Sierra Norte: El Pedroso

El Pedroso is just a tiny village that most people drive through on the way to the National Park, but it's worth stopping here if you're a hearty carnivore. There are surprisingly few specialist game outlets in the region, but **Nortecaza**, located on the roundabout just outside El Pedroso as you head for Seville, is one of them. It's a combined butcher's, meat processing factory, restaurant and tapas bar. Local hunters supply the rabbit, hare, boar, venison, partridge and deer, and it also makes chorizos and patés.

Sierra Subbética: Rute

Rute, snuggled against the southern edge of Sierra Subbética Natural Park in Córdoba province, is one of those attractive agricultural towns where the dogs still snooze in the road and no-one minds if you're driving at 20 kilometres an hour because you're lost – it's just tractor speed, after all. The town was, and is, a centre for anise liqueur production, although there are now only five distilleries still operating. They have all had to diversify from the original *aguardiente* to flavoured, sweetened, less alcoholic spirits to suit modern tastes. The Duende distillery, founded in 1908, opened its **Museo del Anis** (Paseo del Fresno 2; tel: 957 538 143) in 1995 as a way of attracting visitors. It is an educational centre combined with a tasting area, and of course a shop where you can buy attractively packaged anise in myriad permutations. Try the chocolate or hazelnut versions: I think they'd slip down a treat after a snowy walk, and are wonderful poured over vanilla ice cream. The centre is open Monday to Friday, 9am to 2pm and 4pm to 7pm; weekends from 8am to 3pm; and during the summer months, in the mornings only.

Head next door to stock up on Christmas sweeties at **La Flor de Rute**, which has also set up a **Museo del Mantecado** (C Málaga 21). Rute seems to be Museo-mad, because on the other side of the square is the **Museo de Jamón** (C Loja 15; tel: 957 539 227). The front porch contains a plaque with the words of the writer Miguel Cervantes, who in one of his stories prescribes the hams of Rute as an excellent cure-all. The museum is run by the brothers Jiménez and devotes several rooms to displaying ham-curing and sausage-making artefacts. It is a tribute to their father, Pablo Jiménez, who worked for 60 years as butcher and sausage-maker. This honourable tradition continues, and the meat counter is piled high with hand-made croquettes, hams, chorizos and sausages. The *morcilla blanca* is particularly delicious. The shop also stocks other groceries, including cookies; the local varieties, unsurprisingly, contain anise.

Bread and biscuits

Bread, or *pan* in Spanish, simply goes hand in hand with eating in Andalucía, which is the only Spanish region where more than half the population eat bread for breakfast. And not only is it present at every meal, but many of the famous dishes of the region have bread as a major ingredient.

Bread uses

Lots of recipes specify *una rebanada de pan del dia anterior* – a slice of yesterday's bread. Andalucians endured severe hardship and poverty until a couple of generations ago, the culinary consequence of which is that cooks are still able to magic delicious food out of very little, and nothing is ever wasted, including stale bread. Indeed, Carmen Ladrón from La Cartuja de Cazalla has memories from her childhood of bread actually being the whole meal. In winter, pieces would be toasted over an open fire using olive twigs as a toasting fork, and sometimes travellers would arrive with their loaves, asking for some olive oil to pour into the hollowed-out centre, with the cut-away crust doing duty as a stopper.

Bread, sometimes toasted, is frequently ground up (traditionally in a pestle and mortar) with other ingredients and used to thicken sauces. Indeed, there are some recipes that require up to half a loaf, gazpacho being the classic example. Less well-known is *ajo colorado*, literally "red garlic", a dish popular for Christmas and in Holy Week, made with lots of garlic, paprika, breadcrumbs, oil and lemon, and salt-cod.

Migas doesn't sound promising: stale bread, either in pieces or in crumbs, soaked in water, then fried in olive oil and garlic, with the addition of other ingredients like green peppers, *chorizo*, *longaniza*, *panceta* and *morcilla*. But actually, it's very rich and very more-ish: do try it if you get the chance.

And where would the Andalucian tapas bars be without bread? Many hot tapas come with a hunk of bread, while cold tapas are routinely served with bread sticks called *picos* – which look like tiny croissants but are very dry and incredibly noisy to eat.

At home, bread is bought fresh, daily – sometimes twice a day – from a *panadería*, a term that refers to a bread shop or bakery, although in some villages you may see a sign *despacho de pan*, which literally means "bread office": this is a small shop attached to the bakery, selling their bread direct to their customers.

Bread styles

Though bread comes in all kinds of shapes, sizes and types (in some places you can buy large round loaves weighing up to three kilos), the most commonly bought bread is a *barra*, which is generally shaped much like a baguette but can be any longish loaf of white bread. And it can be just half a loaf, *media barra*: bakeries and bread shops are very happy to cut a loaf in half for you. *Pan molde* is UK-style soft white sliced bread, and *pan integral* is brown or wholemeal bread.

Some of the best breads in Andalucía are those that have been made in traditional wood-fired ovens, *hornos de leña*, which produce a really firm and crusty loaf. Most bakeries use electric or gas-fired ovens these days to make the country-style *pan rústico* or *pan de pueblo*, and it just isn't quite as delicious as a loaf from the *horno de leña*.

Gazpacho

For most of its history, gazpacho was a simple peasant dish of garlic, vinegar, olive oil and bread. The suffix *-acho* is a derogatory one, so it's fairly clear that this soup was looked down on as rather humble food.

Even after the tomato and the pepper were imported from the Americas, it was still a couple of centuries before gazpacho recipes started to mention them. Even in 1747 the Spanish writer Juan de la Mata's recipe did not yet list tomato, pepper or cucumber. European visitors in the first half of the nineteenth century do mention peppers and cucumber among the ingredients for gazpacho, but still not tomatoes. It wasn't until around 1880 that red gazpacho as we know it began to show up.

In fact, gazpacho was a workman's snack: it was made in the fields using a pestle and mortar and then popped down the nearest well to keep cool. The soup would be drunk at intervals through the day. The notion of drinking gazpacho still continues, and you'll often find it served in a bowl with handles, although these days a spoon is always provided.

Gazpacho really refers to a whole family of soups that can be red, green or white, depending on the vegetables and herbs that are added, although the basic ingredients of garlic, bread, oil and vinegar are always the same – well, mostly. As you may have realised, it's never that straightforward in Andalucía. In Jaén, for example, and in some other parts of Spain, *gazpachos pastorales* are game soups made by shepherds, where the bread is cooked separately and

added later to the pot.

It's the chilled red gazpacho soup we're all familiar with – made with tomatoes, green peppers and cucumber. Sometimes the cucumber is kept back as a garnish, along with the other usual accompaniments of chopped *jamón* and hard-boiled egg. In Antequera, the green peppers are substituted with red, and paprika is often an extra ingredient.

Salmorejo, or *porra*, is a cream-consistency gazpacho, made without the water, and it originates from Córdoba and Antequera.

Green gazpachos typically originate from Huelva. Here the extra ingredients can include leaf coriander, mint, parsley, basil, green salad leaves and cucumber.

White gazpachos derive their colour from the use of ground nuts, usually almonds, as is the case with Málaga's *ajo blanco*. Occasionally pine nuts are used instead – this is typical of Córdoba, in fact – and there's even a recipe that calls for ground dried broad beans.

Gazpachuelo, which originates from Málaga, is a sort of thinned-down mayonnaise, to which potatoes, clams, peeled prawns, white fish or boiled eggs may be added.

But in true Andalucian style, there is no set recipe for any of them, so you'll have to learn to trust your taste buds. Whatever variation you come up with, try to remember that you're looking for a harmonious blend of flavours, rather than a soup tasting predominantly of say, green pepper, to the detriment of the tomato.

There are some smaller snack and sandwich breads too:

bollo is a (usually soft) roll; and a *rosca* or *rosquilla* is a ring-shaped form, a bit like a bagel

chapata is ciabatta-like in texture, rectangular and with a firm crust.

mollete is a soft oval roll, originally from Antequera in Málaga, and traditionally eaten for breakfast. It's either heated in the oven or lightly toasted, and then drizzled with olive oil or buttered; sometimes it's eaten with tomato and oil put through a blender, or spread with a pork-and-seasoning mixture like chicharrones.

Speciality breads

Look out for local specialities: for example *salaílla*, a type of bread from the Albaicín district of Granada. This is a round, flat, firm bread with a scattering of salt crystals in the crust: hence its name, which means "salty".

In Úbeda, you'll find an orange-coloured bread, flavoured with paprika and salt, called *ochio*. And during Easter week here people eat a curious hat-shaped bread called *hornazo*, which has a hard-boiled egg in the centre.

Biscuits and pastries

Cast your eyes round any Andalucian bakery, deli or corner grocery store and you'll notice bags, boxes and trays of biscuits, sweets and pastries, piled high on every available flat surface. There is usually a blizzard of icing sugar covering these sweetmeats, and it's not only there for decorative purposes but also to satisfy the legendary sweet tooth of Andalucians. Not just for biscuits, either: puddings such as *angelorum* or *bienmesabe* (which children say looks like squashed toad, but is in fact a mixture of cinnamon, sugar and grounds almonds) are also intensely sweet.

Of course, biscuits, cakes and pastries are gastronomic specialities all over Spain, but the tradition of making sweet things is particularly strong in Andalucía, thanks to all those centuries of Moorish rule and the Arabic love of sweets. It is an irony, perhaps, that this old Arabic tradition – along with other ancient sweet-making arts which had their roots in the large Jewish communities who once lived in Andalucía – was quietly nurtured and maintained, after the purges, by the Christian convents and monasteries, who even now employ the same centuries-old and sometimes secret recipes.

Curiously, the sherry industry also played an important role in feeding the collective sweet tooth, by donating egg yolks to the convents. Egg whites were an important item, used for clarifying sherry, but yolks were superfluous to requirements. So the nuns were able to transform them into puddings and cakes and biscuits, which they either presented to their benefactors, or sold to the public. In fact, when their lands were confiscated in the nineteenth century, many convents turned to baking as a central source of income.

As a consequence, Andalucian sweets do have some wonderfully evocative names: Nun's Sighs, *suspiros de monja*, are sugar-dusted fried pastries; Heavenly Bacon, *tocino de cielo*, is a dense, super-sweet, cinnamon-swirled version of creme caramel; Angel's Hair, *cabello de ángel*, is a highly-sugared, slightly stringy-textured pumpkin jam often used as a pastry filling; and there's a gorgeous biscuit delightfully named Bishop's Tongue, *lengua de obispo*.

Today there may be fewer convents, but huge quantities of their cookies, in hundreds of different varieties, are still eaten at Christmas, New Year and Easter – or just enjoyed with a cup of coffee to celebrate a special occasion.

Pastry pilgrimages

Buying something from one of the convents and monasteries scattered across Andalucía is akin to a pilgrimage for the devout visiting foodie. Never mind the reward: just do it for the experience, because it is quite unlike any other shopping you are likely to do in Andalucía – or anywhere else, for that matter.

The first challenge is actually finding the convent or monastery (it will rarely be signposted); the second is making sure you get there when it's open. And then there is the ritual greeting to remember. Traditionally the nun will greet you with: *Ave María purísima* (hail Virgin Mary), to which your reply should be: *Sin pecado concebida* (conceived without sin). Only then do you

get to ask her for what you'd like, and to place your money on the wooden revolving shelf. There will be a whirl, and off your euros go, into another, holier, world; and then, another whirl, and your biscuits or sweets will appear. Don't fret – change is always given. Incidentally, when you present yourself at the counter in the wall, you may not be able to see the wimpled figure serving you. These convents and monasteries are often enclosed orders, whose inmates are to have no direct contact with the outside world.

Some convents sell their goodies all year round, others just at Christmas time. And when you ask about buying convent sweets, *dulces de convento,* you may well be directed to a *monasterio*, which in Spanish means convent as well as monastery.

Variations on a theme

Classifying all the sweets available is simply impossible, as nearly everyone has their own version of every recipe. The basic ingredients, obviously, are flour, sugar, fat and flavourings. Sometimes eggs and ground almonds are added. The fat may be lard, in which case the mixture is always baked; if olive oil is used then the goodies may also be fried. As for flavourings, the most common ones are anise, sesame seeds, cinnamon, lemon and orange peel, and wine. But most convents have their own specialities, and there are always variations on all the basic recipes, with ingredients being added to adapt the flavouring of many of the most common cakes, sweets and biscuits.

Still, here are some of the most popular and widely available sweet biscuits and pastries you are likely to come across.

Alfajores are biscuits made with almonds,

sugar, and usually cloves, but often other spices and flavourings.

Mantecados and *polvorones* are crumbly little biscuits, *mantecados* being the firmer of the two. They often come individually wrapped in paper, because they do tend to crumble all over the place, and they are made from lard and almonds, flavoured with cinnamon and sesame, and dusted with icing sugar.

Mazapanes are shaped pieces of marzipan, the paste made from ground almonds and sugar. The tradition of marzipan-making goes back directly to the Arabs, who called this sweetmeat *maysaban*, and it later entered Jewish cuisine as *massapan*. Although it's a convent speciality in Andalucía, the origins of marzipan really lie outside the region: the nuns of the Convent of Saint Clement in Toledo, 70 km south-west of Madrid, claim to have first made marzipan in 1212, when they ran out of bread and only had almonds and sugar left in the larder.

Mostachones are biscuits which in some places are S-shaped. You put two biscuits together and you have a moustache – hence the name.

Pastas de almendras are almond biscuits; *pastitas* are smaller biscuits in different shapes.

Pastel de cabello de ángel is a pastry made with *cabello de ángel* or *cidra confitada* – a conserve made from the citron melon, or spaghetti squash, a type of pumpkin.

Pestiños and *borrachuelos* are great favourites at Easter, although they are available all year round. These fried pastries are also called *dulces de sartén*, which literally means frying-pan sweets, and they are usually flavoured with aniseed or cinnamon, although you'll also find variations using orange juice, sweet white wine, sherry or anise liqueur. Whatever the flavourings, they are always dipped in honey before being dusted with sugar.

Roscos, or *rosquillos*, are rings of dough which are either baked or fried and then dusted with sugar. *Roscos de vino* contain wine as a flavouring, and *roscos de anis*, anise liqueur.

Soplillos are meringues made with crushed almonds.

Yemas are candied egg yolks, and are made by gently cooking an egg yolk mixture in sugar syrup; *tocino de cielo* is similarly made from little more than sugar, water and eggs.

Nevertheless, the crunchiest, crumbliest, most delicious of all the biscuits you can buy

are *tortas de aceite*. These are very thin, saucer-sized confections made with anise, flour, olive oil, sugar and sesame seeds, which are baked and then individually wrapped in greaseproof paper. Sometimes chopped almonds are scattered over the top, but to be honest this embellishment verges on gilding the lily – they're totally delicious as they are.

Biscuit business

Of course, convents and monasteries aren't the only producers of pastries and biscuits. One very well-known brand found all over Spain is Ines Rosales. This is a family-run business based just outside Seville. Their range of cookies include *tortas de aceite*, *polvorones* and *pestiños* – and they are all hand-made, usually from locally-sourced ingredients. It takes 6 months, apparently, to train people to flatten the dough patties properly: experienced workers shape over twenty tortas a minute. The company also has a policy of employing teams of disabled workers.

Some towns are famous for their biscuit-making. Rute is one (see page 45), and Estepa and Medina Sidonia are two others, where in the run-up to Christmas the whole town seems to smell of baking. Medina Sidonia claims to be the pastry capital of the province of Cádiz: the cakes and biscuits produced here include *tortas pardas* (almond-based pastry filled with *amarguillos*, a sweetmeat made with both sweet and bitter almonds), *piñonates* (pine nut cakes), along with the more usual *polvorones*, *mantecados* and *pestiños*. However, the town is most famous for its *alfajores*, cylindrical in shape, with a characteristic tang of coriander – although the exact recipe for this pastry is a secret closely guarded by the Agrupación de Productores de Alfajores de Medina Sidonia.

Rute is one (see page 45)

Convents to visit
Here is a selection of Andalucian convents and monasteries whose goodies are particularly worth seeking out:

Granada
Monasterio de San Bernardo (C Gloria 2) sells a large selection of different sweets and biscuits over the Christmas period. For the rest of the year their selection is more limited but you can usually buy a *caja surtida*, a selection of their range. Do what many locals do: buy a box, take it to a nearby café, and enjoy with a cup of coffee.

Seville
Monasterio Jerónimo de Santa Paula (C Santa Paula 56) specialises in delicious jams and conserves including orange, fig and quince. It keeps the same opening hours as its museum, 10.30am to 12.30pm and 4.30pm to 6.30pm, but closed on Mondays.
Convento de San Leandro (Plaza de San Leandro 1) are famous for their yemas, one of the most typical sweets eaten in Seville. These and other cakes baked by the nuns can be bought during normal business hours inside the convent.
Convento de Santa Ines (C Doña María Coronel s/n) contains the remains of its founder, Doña María Coronel, a Sevillian noblewoman courted by King Pedro the Cruel. Legend tells of how Doña María disfigured herself with boiling oil to deter the persistent amorous advances of the king, who even had her husband executed as part of his campaign to woo her. A less extreme avoidance tactic might have been just to eat vast quantities of the convent's delicious cakes.

Store cupboard staples

Walk into any Andalucian grocery store and you very quickly realise that here is your chance to turn your store cupboard into a veritable Aladdin's cave of delectable goodies. In addition to all the basics, you'll also find a quite dazzling array of tinned and bottled fish, meat, fruit and vegetables.

Hold on. Tinned produce? Are you raising an eyebrow? For the British in particular, tinned food is often seen as rather second-class in terms of quality – with the exception of a certain brand of baked beans, of course.

Well, in Spain it is the other way round: produce that has a short season tends to be considered a delicacy, and is put into tins for year-round consumption. Prime examples range from the everyday to the esoteric: white asparagus, tuna belly, cod cheeks, partridge *en escabeche,* and *piquillo* peppers.

The latter are slightly piquant and ready grilled and peeled. They are so good tinned, in fact, that no-one ever really bothers to buy them fresh, especially if they are going to be stuffed.

Chocolate

Hot chocolate and *churros*, thin doughnut rings, is a never-mind-the-calories classic combo you should try at least once in your visit. It is traditionally indulged in after a night's revelling as a sort of very early breakfast. The drink is made by melting pieces of chocolate and adding milk, so it's deliciously rich and thick. This is about the only use of chocolate in Andaluz cookery, unlike in Catalonia and the Basque regions where chocolate is also used in savoury sauces.

Columbus, with his Andalucian and Basque crew, didn't fully appreciate the potential of chocolate when he came across the beans on his third voyage to the New World. It

was in fact Cortés and his *conquistadores*, after they had invaded Mexico, who learned to love the frothy black beverage. It was rumoured by the Spanish to be an aphrodisiac, and addictive (especially for women) even then – so much so, that its reputation arrived in Europe well before the *cacao* itself. Chocolate-making was a secret of the Spanish monasteries for ages; and in the seventeenth century the Spanish court was famed throughout Europe for its wonderful chocolate drinks. It's no surprise then that the habit has continued.

Food colouring

Plenty of local cooks simply swear by food colouring, *colorante alimentario*, to add vibrancy – often as a substitute for saffron – to their soups, stews and casseroles. It's so popular that boxes or little envelopes of yellow powder can be bought even in the remotest village shops.

Honey

The honeys from the sierras are fabulous, and they are not all based on thyme or spring flowers. The bees collect nectar from some unusual blooms such as chestnut blossom and eucalyptus flowers. Honey, *miel*, also finds its way into many biscuits, as well as being added to some savoury dishes: roast lamb with almonds always has honey added, true to its Moorish origins.

Noodles

There are not many pasta dishes in traditional Andalucian cuisine. But an exception is *gurullos,* tiny rice-shaped pasta that are traditional to Almería (see page 126 for a recipe). *Fideos* are short noodles, which sometimes find their way into some of the region's traditional soups.

Olives

Most Spanish olives, *aceitunas*, are picked green, before they ripen and fall from the tree. These green olives are very bitter, and need to be soaked in water and brine for some time before they are edible. There are two main varieties of green table olive produced in Andalucía: the large *gordal*, or queen olive, which is usually eaten as a tapa, dressed in olive oil; and the smaller *manzanilla*, the most common eating olive, which is frequently used in salads. In bars and markets, green olives are available *aliñadas* – marinaded in vinegar, spices and herbs.

Black olives are less common in Andalucía, but it is worth looking out for the small dried black olives which can be found in some markets and specialist shops.

Olive oil

More oil is produced in Spain than any other country in Europe, and Andalucía is Spain's main olive-growing area with over 150 million trees. Amazingly, this accounts for nearly 20% of global production. So it's no surprise that frying is a popular method of cooking, or that olive oil, *aceite de oliva*, gets used in everything from biscuits to shampoo.

Aceite de Oliva Virgen Extra (extra virgin) is cold pressed: it's produced from crushed olives, using mechanical methods only, and without using high temperatures or solvents to extract the oil. It is the best quality oil, with the most flavour and the lowest acidity (no more than one per cent).

Aceite de Oliva is a blend of refined and cold pressed oil; this is the standard oil – the one people use for most purposes.

The main varieties of oil-producing olives cultivated in Andalucía are: the *picual*, which produces a peppery oil which goes well with salads containing oranges, and is a popular oil for frying; the *hojiblanca*, which gives a nutty oil with a slightly bitter tang; and the *verdial*, mostly grown in Málaga, which produces a mild-flavoured oil.

Denominación de Origen Olive oils

Given olive oil's importance, it is no surprise to find that there are several olive oil DOs in the region.

Sierra de Cazorla, **Sierra Magina**, and **Sierra de Segura** are three DOs from Jaén province, which produces almost half of Andalucía's olive oil, with roughly 560,000 hectares growing olive trees. The *picual* olive is the main variety grown here, along with a tiny amount of a variety called *royal* that is most commonly found in the Sierra de Cazorla. The olives are harvested slightly green, and the resulting oil is fruity, slightly bitter, and varying in colour from deep green to golden yellow, depending on when the olives were harvested. There are many organic producers: Verde Salud is often considered to be the best in the area.

Montes de Granada is an olive-growing area in the province of Granada, producing a very aromatic, slightly bitter, green to greenish-yellow oil. Again, most of the olives used are of the *picual* variety; and the olives have to be harvested directly from the tree to be accredited with the DO label.

Sierra de Cádiz is the most recent area to achieve DO status. There's a bigger mix of olive varieties here, and in fact a lesser-known variety called *lechin* accounts for half the olives grown. The colour of the oil varies between deep green and golden

Peppers

Pimientos secos are a festive sight, garlanding balconies and outhouses in the autumn. If you want to buy some, you'll find vegetable stalls in the local market of any rural town in the sierras, bedecked like Santa's Grotto with hundreds of whole dried pepper strings hanging from the ceiling.

When ground, they give colour to chorizos and sausages; they are often also added to meat casseroles, and soups or stews

yellow, with a fruity fragrance and a slightly peppery flavour.

Baena, south of Córdoba, is probably the best-known of the olive oil producing regions, largely thanks to one producer: Nuñez de Prado. This family has been producing olive oil on their estate for over 200 years. They are most famous for their *Flor de Aceite*, which is considered one of Spain's very best. *Flor* is actually the name given to free-run, unpressed oil: the olives are crushed, and then put into a rotating cylinder lined with fine mesh; think of a washing machine on very slow spin – the fruit simply seeps the oil out, thanks to its own weight and the force of gravity. This cloudy oil is organic, unpressed and unfiltered, which makes it about as unprocessed as it is possible for an olive oil to be. It's got a sweet tropical fruit aroma, and a slightly almondy taste with a hint of pepper.

Non-DO Olive oils

Molino de San Nicolás y San Esteban is an example of a great olive oil to be found in a non-DO area. It's a small operation, only 26 hectares, situated a few kilometres outside the town of Beas in the province of Huelva. But the manager, Nicolás Gómez Martín, and his team pay careful attention to the details – with the result that the mill smells just like ... olive oil. (And if you're thinking "well, obviously", then just wind down your car window next time you pass by a large automated oil mill and catch a whiff of the pungent, slightly rancid odour.) It's the little things that make all the difference: to maintain freshness, the olives are picked green; and they're picked either by hand, or with a hand-held vibrating clamp – no beating of the trees here, as this would damage the branches. Next, the olives are handled very carefully: they're washed with non-chlorinated water, and milled without heating or the addition of talc or water, which is the industry norm. And the oil is extracted only on alternate days, allowing time for the machinery to be cleaned properly.

Three olive varieties are used: *arbequina*, *hojiblanca* and *picual*, in a ratio of approximately 50-30-20. The *arbequina*, a variety more popular in Catalonia, gives the aroma; the *hojiblanca* contributes smoothness; and the *picual* gives the oil stability, as well as its subtle peppery finish. Nicolás mills these varieties separately. The oils are never blended until each has been tested in his laboratory to determine how smooth and how bitter it is.

Last year, they produced just under 11,000 litres of oil. Not only does it have lovely green smells of cut grass, raw almonds, and apples, but the flavour is fat and smooth with a slightly peppery finish, and it lingers in your mouth for a long time like a fine wine. It's truly gorgeous stuff: buy some if you can (see page 31 for one outlet).

containing chickpeas or dried beans. For good measure, half a dried pepper is sometimes added as a garnish, and it's good to eat, too: a bit like nibbling on a sweet pepper crisp. To use dried peppers, split open, rinse, and remove stalks and seeds before adding to the dish. They tend to break down during cooking: some cooks remove them when they've turned soft, and blend them with a mouli-mill into just a little of the cooking liquid, returning the resulting salsa to the pan just before serving.

Rice

Think of a Spanish rice dish, and most people will immediately conjure visions of *paella*, which originates from Valencia. But actually, more rice, *arroz*, is grown in the province of Seville than anywhere else in Spain. In fact, the area around the town of Villafranca del Guadalquivir, halfway between Seville and the coast, grows roughly half of Spain's crop.

Rice, Andaluz-style

Willy Moya is the owner-chef of Seville's only specialist rice restaurant, La Cartuja. Here's the benefit of his advice on Andaluz rice dishes – and how they differ from paella.

Wet rice, dry rice

Paella gets its name from the shallow pan, *paellera*, that it's made in, and rice is certainly the fundamental ingredient in this dish. To be cooked perfectly, all the moisture has to be absorbed by the rice – in other words, paella belongs to the family of dry-rice dishes. To ensure there's no leftover liquid, the cook has to be absolutely precise with the quantities of stock and rice. What's more, the timing has to be spot-on too, because perfect paella is always eaten *al dente*. (Incidentally, it's for this reason that onion shouldn't be used in paella, as it would soften the rice.)

By contrast, Andaluz rice dishes are invariably moist, almost soupy: even dishes that might seem to be in the paella style should still keep some liquid in them. On the whole, these wet-rice dishes tend to be cooked in a general-purpose pot, and rice is just one part of the composite whole, not the key ingredient. Also, things can easily find themselves being added to an Andaluz rice dish – so the quantities really don't have to be too exact.

To stir or not to stir

When you make paella, the ingredients are fried first; water or stock is then added, followed finally by the rice. In Andaluz dishes, the rice is always added to the other ingredients that are being fried, before any water or stock is added.

With paella, once the rice is in the pan, the mixture is not touched until it is ready to be served. This ensures that no starch is separated from the rice. For the first five minutes the paella is allowed to simmer on a fairly high heat, which tends to make the rice stick to the bottom and get slightly burnt – the best bit for many people. But after that, the heat is lowered and the dish is left to cook by itself.

In the more soupy Andaluz dishes, short-grained rice, *arroz bomba*, with its high starch content, is a favourite for thickening the juice or stock, and stirring is allowed (though not too much, as you don't want *all* the starch to separate from the rice).

Many farming families moved here from Valencia during and after the civil war, and it was they that developed the production of long-grain rice, most of which is exported these days. Typically, most Andaluz rice dishes still tend to favour the shorter-grained rice that originally grew in the region.

Sugar cane

Sugar cane, *caña de azúcar*, was probably first introduced here by the Carthaginians, but it has certainly been in continuous cultivation along parts of Granada's Costa Tropical ever since the Arabs arrived and started to refine the stuff. In fact, the area around Motril is sometimes referred to as Little Cuba thanks to the sugar cane that is still grown there. The cane is also turned into molasses, *miel de caña*. This is not only used in sweet dishes, but sometimes poured onto deep-fried aubergines and fritters of tiny prawns, *tortillitas de camarón*.

Vinegar

As anyone knows who has let an opened bottle of wine hang around for a couple of weeks, the contents doesn't necessarily turn into vinegar, or *vinagre* in Spanish – it often merely tastes nasty. The scientific process of turning alcohol into acetic acid requires not just any old bacteria to munch away at it, but a particular culture called *Acetobacter aceti*, which is present in the air, but which may or may not choose to get involved at any given moment.

When *A.aceti* did occasionally sneak in between the wine and the barrel at the sherry bodegas in Cádiz province, it was generally regarded as an unwelcome

Cooking times vary too. You generally need to allow 16-18 minutes once you've added rice to a paella. After this, you should remove the paella pan from the heat, and cover the rice with a tea towel for 5-10 minutes to ensure that it fully absorbs any remaining excess moisture. Of course, the dish then gets eaten straight away, but that's usually more to do with people being hungry – paella won't spoil if you leave it a while. An Andaluz rice dish will typically get a few minutes more cooking time than a paella, but once it's ready, it should be eaten immediately. A stodgy *arroz* pudding is not what you're aiming at here.

Andaluz cuisine sees rice being put together with just about anything. But typical dishes are *arroz con perdiz* (rice with partridge), *arroz con conejo* (rice with rabbit), *arroz con pato* (rice with duck), and *arroz con mariscos* (rice with shellfish).

Slightly less typical is *arroz del señorito*, made with seafood in a similar way to paella, and using a *paellera*, but nevertheless still slightly moist. And with *arroz con bacalao* (rice with salt-cod), the stock is brought to the boil in the pot and then transferred to the oven to finish cooking.

intrusion. But what a difference a gastronomic revival can make. Nowadays, *Vinagre de Jerez* has its own Denominación de Origen (DO), and most bodegas have a flourishing sideline making it, albeit in small quantities.

It's made in the same way as sherry: the solera system (see page 90) is a process that is also ideally suited to vinegar production, because it takes such a long time for the alcohol to be converted. The result is an absolutely gorgeous condiment with a very intense aromatic taste that is quite unlike its vulgar –

some might say yobbish – cousin, malt vinegar. They also have a vinegar DO in Huelva, by the way: *DO Vinagre del Condado de Huelva*, the best examples of which are made in the same way as those in Jerez. And the only other vinegar DO in the world is Modena in Italy, where those balsamic vinegars are produced.

By and large, there are two main culinary uses for sherry vinegar – and vinegars in general. First, as a flavour enhancer: it has the happy capacity to lift flavours, in much the same way that lemon juice does, and a few drops are all that is needed. In Andalucía, cooks use sherry vinegar to add to their gazpachos and their salads; and it is especially wonderful when added to lentil stew.

The other use for vinegar is as a preservative. Winters aren't severe here, so there has never been much need to pickle vegetables in Andalucía – but making the most of a glut of small fish such as sardines is another matter, especially when it's 40 degrees outside. The word *escabeche* is one that you will see quite a lot on menus, and it refers to the vinegar mixture used to pickle both fish and game.

The Romans used vinegar as a thirst quencher, curiously, and this may be why it is one of the ingredients in a very early version of gazpacho that consisted of bread and vinegar.

Finally, a note of warning: the strength of vinegar is rarely specified in recipes, and vinegars can vary in concentration from 4% up to around 9% acetic acid – *Vinagre de Jerez* has a minimum of 7%. There are wide differences in flavours, too. So proceed with caution. It's always easier to add more later, than it is to figure out what to do with an over-vinegared dish, other than to bin it.

Fridge essentials

Cheese

Cheese, *queso*, is enormously popular throughout Spain. Ask people to name a Spanish cheese, and most will reply *manchego*, an absolutely delicious sheep's milk cheese that is sold at varying degrees of maturity: the older it is, the more pungent and nutty it becomes. Once upon a time, in the days before pasteurisation, travelling cheese-sellers would hawk their sacks of *manchego* cheeses around the homes and villages, and housewives would have to judge the cheeses rather carefully – if they hadn't been looked after properly, their families might end up with tummy troubles.

These days, despite the popularity of *manchego*, sheep's milk doesn't actually account for most of Spain's cheese. Mostly it's blended in with cow's milk and goat's milk. And the blend will determine the character of the cheese. Generally speaking, cow's milk provides bulk and flavour; goat's milk adds whiteness and also provides the tart zesty notes; and sheep's milk gives a nutty, rich, butteriness. In most people's view, the more sheep's milk, the better the cheese.

Andalucía certainly isn't cow country, so the cheeses here are mostly sheep's milk or goat's milk anyway, and you'll find a surprising variety of cheeses that are more or less unknown outside the region. Many of them are simple artisan products made at home by shepherds and farmers, and happily devoured more or less on the spot by appreciative locals. Some of them, though, are made in sufficient quantities to find their way into the shops occasionally, so look out for these:

Queso Alpujarreño

This is made in the Alpujarras in the provinces of Granada and Almería from goat's milk. It is fairly mild to taste, with a buttery texture. You can sometimes buy it rolled in rosemary.

Incidentally, if you're over in the Lecrín valley, there's a good organic cheese shop, or *quesería*, in Padul called Los Teatinos (C Gustavo Adolfo Bécquer 8) who sell fresh and cured goat's milk cheese.

Queso de Aracena

This is also a goat's milk cheese, from the Sierra de Aracena, and it has a strong and piquant flavour. Sometimes it's cured with a covering of olive oil, although you can also buy it fresh – in which case it will have a milder taste. One award-winning producer to look out for is La Finca Los Robledos. And in José Vicente's restaurant in Aracena (Av de Andalucía 53; tel: 959 128 455), they serve a salad of tomatoes and the local cured cheese with a simple dressing of olive and vinegar. For lovers of goat's cheese, this is a sublime experience.

Queso de la Calahorra

This is produced in the province of Granada. It's a strong, creamy cheese made either from sheep's milk or a mixture of sheep's milk and goat's milk.

Queso de Grazalema

Grazalema is one of the White Towns of Cádiz province, and its sheep's milk cheese is very similar to *manchego* in texture and taste. It keeps quite well too: up to a year in a cool place.

Queso de Los Pedroches

This is a sheep's milk cheese made in the Pedroches valley in Córdoba province. It's semi-hard, quite strong-tasting, and ready for eating after a month or two, though if you pop it into olive oil it will keep for longer.

Queso de Cabra de Málaga

A goat's milk cheese from the mountainous part of Málaga province. For those of you who don't like your cheese too strong, this is

Sierra de Cazorla

a good one to choose, as it's mild and creamy. It will keep for two to three months.

Queso Fresco de Cabra de Cádiz

Fresh cheese, *queso fresco*, tends to be mild and bland, and needs to be combined with something sweet or salty. This one is delightful eaten with quince paste, or dried fruit, or as part of a salad.

You should definitely also keep an eye out for *los Balanchares*. These are baby cheeses, oven-baked, produced by Quesería de la Sierra Subbética in Zuheros, Córdoba. Usually sold in vacuum packs of two cheeses, they make a delicious supper. Just sprinkle herbs (thyme or oregano) and a little olive oil over each cheese, before baking them in a moderate oven until they start to melt. Then simply cut off small pieces and spread on bread or toast: yum.

Finally, here are a few terms you might come across on cheese labels:

queso de cabra: goat's cheese
queso de oveja: ewe's cheese
queso fresco: fresh cheese
requesón: fresh curd cheese
queso tierno: cheese which is slightly matured but still soft and mild
semi-curado: cheese that's cured for about a month
curado: cured for three months, drier in texture and stronger-tasting.

Eggs

Eggs, or *huevos*, are a Spanish institution. Apart from fabulous fried eggs (see box on page 58), the Spanish are also utterly brilliant at scrambled eggs and omelettes – and somehow these prosaic terms simply don't do their dishes justice.

Anyway, *huevos revueltos* are the scrambled eggs. This is a great way of making a small amount of an expensive or scarce ingredient go further, while at the same time transforming a humble food into something sensuous and sophisticated – so it's very, very Andalucian. For example, in springtime you might see young garlic shoots mixed into the eggs.

And *tortilla* is the omelette, though it isn't like a French omelette at all. The name actually means "little cake", and a *tortilla* should be thick enough and solid enough to cut into cubes or slices. It shouldn't really be eaten hot, either: much better to have it warm, or even at room temperature, as the flavour improves as it cools.

One of the most common tortillas is *tortilla española,* which uses three fairly ordinary ingredients – eggs, onion and potato – and

somehow conjures up a dish that's rather luxurious. It's often served as a *tapa* – and in Seville, you may come across it refried in oil, garlic and whisky.

If you're going to have a go at creating your own tortilla, then just remember that the volume of the eggs should be roughly equal to the volume of the vegetables or meat. Take at least 20 minutes to sauté these ingredients, which should always be raw – never use boiled potatoes, for example – before removing them to add into the beaten eggs. Don't ever just add the eggs into the frying-pan mixture: you may think you're saving time, but I promise you it'll all end up as egg mash. And the tortilla will need to be turned halfway through cooking. If flipping isn't your thing – and it does take a deft wrist (and a slug or two of sherry for cook's courage) – then you can always cheat by placing the pan under a heated grill.

As God intended

Carmen Ladrón is the owner and restorer of La Cartuja de Cazalla (see page 146), and this tale of hers about eggs struck me as a classic example of the Andalucian approach to food.

Carmen's great-grandmother had been whisked off into marriage at the tender age of thirteen, by a middle-aged man (well, he was 35) who promised that he would teach her to cook eggs, *como Dios manda* – as God intended. The young girl's mother, somewhat peeved that the man hadn't chosen to marry her instead, relented and let her go. Generations later, this little piece of family history was still being recounted in the family kitchen, but since she had no interest in cooking Carmen had never bothered to find out exactly what

the recipe involved.

Well, one night many years later at La Cartuja, two gentlemen pitched up, at about 11 o'clock at night, asking for rooms and something to eat. "The cook has gone home," Carmen demurred, but the men implored her at least to fry them some eggs – after all, they reasoned, in Andalucía everything is fried, isn't it, and being tucked away in the sierras she's bound to keep the odd few chickens. Always hospitable, if no great chef, Carmen set about the task.

She took a small pan, filled it with olive oil, heated the oil until it shimmered, broke an egg into a saucer, and sprinkled sea-salt over the yolk (you never do this after the egg is cooked, always before – everyone

La Cartuja de Cazalla mural

knows that). She slid the egg into the oil, not forgetting to shield her eyes, because it will always spit like a scalded cat, and then she cooked the egg just long enough for the edges to go crispy and frilly: literally a couple of seconds. Then she removed it and repeated the process – in Andalucía you never dish up just one egg.

And her visitors were utterly ecstatic. *Huevos, como Dios manda!*

Carmen was amazed: really? She had just been following the method her mother's cook had always used. Oh yes, they assured her. And we should know, we are chefs, from the Basque country – and these eggs are perfect!

So now you know too.

Ham bones

You can get a ham bone, *hueso de jamón*, or *hueso añejo*, from butchers, specialist food shops and delicatessens, and occasionally you'll find them in ready-wrapped packs at the supermarket. In some shops they will be just piled up in trays on top of the counter, but once you've got one home it's a good idea to keep it in the fridge. Sometimes it's a bone from a cured ham, sliced horizontally into rounds; sometimes it's a whole length of bone. It may well be preserved in salt, which you can rinse off or leave on – but if you leave it on, then you won't want to add any extra salt to the pot. A couple of bone pieces, with the addition of a few vegetables and seasonings, will make a delicious stock, and a *hueso de jamón* is absolutely essential for preparing dishes like *sopa de picadillo* or *cocido*.

Milk

Outside the tourist areas it's quite difficult to come by pasteurised milk, which is called *leche fresca* or *leche del día* in Spanish. It goes off very quickly, even if you keep the fridge door religiously closed, and it's probably only worth buying if you're going to finish it on the same day.

Quince jelly

Dulce de membrillo and *carne de membrillo* (quince paste and quince jelly) can be bought in packs, and are best kept in the fridge. They are delicious with cheese, and especially so with the sharper cured cheeses, as well as fresh goat's milk cheeses or soft curd.

Yesterday's bread

In the fridge? Yes. This is *pan que queda del día anterior,* and good supply of it is absolutely invaluable when cooking many Andaluz dishes: it's a principal ingredient of *gazpacho* and many other soups, it's used to make *migas,*

and it's blended with garlic and spices to make a *majado* to flavour stews and casseroles. You certainly cannot be the genuine Andalucian article without it, and the best way to ensure you always have some when you need it, is to leave a loaf of *pan rústico* for a day, then slice it and then freeze the slices.

Meat

People tend to eat a lot of fish and pulses in this part of the world. Of course, meat is eaten too, and especially pork *embutidos*, but they don't go in much for expensive meat, such as steaks. Andalucians will traditionally tend to cook smaller quantities of a cheaper cut, usually mixed with other ingredients to make it go further and give it some character. *Cocidos*, one-pot stews, are a popular example of this kind of cooking.

Beef

Now, who remembers the classic children's book Ferdinand the Bull? It's a gently funny, if slightly subversive, tale of a bull who didn't like to fight. Well, drive through the back roads in the cork-tree countryside of Córdoba and Seville provinces, and suddenly it will seem all very familiar, thanks to the book's brilliant illustrations. For this is cattle-ranching territory, where most of the cows and steers are destined for the pot. But of course, if a farmer rears beef, *ternera*, then the chances are he will also be breeding bulls for the ring.

And all bulls do meet their end in the ring – even those noble beasts who have managed to wound a matador or, occasionally, send one to meet his maker. You might suppose that having won in this way, a bull would be allowed to retire back to his cork-tree, but no, it just doesn't

work like that. The animals are simply butchered, immediately. In Baeza, for example, the abattoir is right next door to the bullring. The meat will go on sale the next day and it has always traditionally been one of the main sources of beef for poorer folk. Surprisingly, the most highly prized part of the animal is also the most humble: the bull's tail. Simmered in red wine or sherry for about three hours, the resulting gelatinous stew, *rabo de toro*, is utterly delicious.

Other common cuts of meat include veal, which features on a lot of restaurant menus, although this generally refers to young beef, rather than calf reared in a crate. Incidentally, those of you who like the idea of walking in Andalucía, take note: calves are frequently congregated into a kind of day nursery, with one or two cows standing guard while the others graze. Woe betide you, if you should

wander between a mum and her baby: these cows have horns, and you'll need to be mighty fleet of foot to avoid an indignant parent.

Chicken

Industrially-produced chickens are now the order of the day everywhere in Europe, but do try and buy free-range, to get the most out of the Andalucian ways of cooking *pollo*. In farming communities, chickens were – and still are – valued for their eggs as a food source, rather than as food themselves. Thus, a chicken went into the pot only on special occasions, or when she had reached the end of her egg-producing days. And the local ways of cooking chicken reflect this: tough but tasty legs from an elderly bird are added to *cocidos*; while spring chickens are fricasseed with delicious sauces made from sherry, almonds and saffron, or from the very best flavoursome tomatoes and masses of garlic.

Game

Nowadays, most game, or *caza*, is in fact from commercial farms, with hares and snails being possibly the only exceptions. Hunting remains a popular activity, but it is remarkably difficult to find meat from this source – if it's not sold to the restaurant trade, it generally goes straight into the hunter's pot or oven.

Kid

The arid conditions of many parts of Andalucía are ideal for goats – wherever you go you will see herds of them roaming round the countryside. Roast kid, *cabrito*, tastes very much like lamb, and is surprisingly tender, but more often you will encounter *choto al ajillo*, which is young goat-meat cut up and fried with heaps of garlic and then served with a sauce.

Lamb

Andalucía produces the best lamb, or *cordero*, in Spain: the Segureño. This breed is found in Seville, Córdoba, Almería and Jaén, but by far the greatest concentrations of flocks are up in the north-east of Granada, around the towns of Baza and Huéscar. The Segureño is apparently well adapted to the irregular rainfall and sparse vegetation of this region – and just as well, too, because no other breeds seem to be able to cope with it for more than five minutes. Anyhow, the pay-off for this bit of natural selection is quite simply the perfect eating lamb: not too fatty, not too strong-tasting, and not too tough either (they're still tender at 14 months). Up in Granada province you'll find lamb on the menu at just about every restaurant, with chops and ribs being roasted, or grilled over hot coals. The roasting is done in deep tins: the lamb is garnished with potatoes, oil, garlic, green peppers, local white or rosé wine, a little tomato, and sometimes a bayleaf or a sprig of thyme or rosemary, and then roasted at a high temperature. The results, I assure you, are heavenly.

Offal

No part of an animal is ever wasted here, and Andalucians certainly aren't squeamish about innards and extremities. Offal, or *despojos*, is a popular buy at the butcher's, and frequently crops up on restaurant menus too.

Tripe, *callos*, which these days generally arrives ready-cleaned from Argentina, often makes an appearance in a stew with chickpeas.

Pigs' trotters, *manos de cerdo*, are usually stewed in a sauce, and can be exceptionally good. Occasionally, the meat is even taken off the trotter, so you're not actually presented with a hoof on a plate. Hooray.

Brains, *sesos*, also turn up from time to time, along with *criadillas de cordero*, lambs' testicles, in what is loudly promoted as the classic omelette dish from Granada: *tortilla de Sacromonte*. This certainly does appear on a large number of tourist menus, but it has to be said that it doesn't seem to be the omelette of choice for most Granadinos.

Also at the butcher's, or on the restaurant menus, you may see: kidneys, *riñones* – the classic recipe is *riñones al jerez*, fried with sherry; also *higado* (liver), *mollejas* (sweetbreads), and *lengua* (tongue).

Partridge

Partridge, or *perdiz*, is traditionally served, sometimes cold, *en escabeche*. This means that the bird is fried first, and then marinated

or slow-cooked in vinegar. Tinned *perdiz en escabeche* is very popular, and you'll find it stocked everywhere. Try it served up with a salad, with lots of chopped tomatoes, spring onions, oregano, olive oil and a few drops of sherry vinegar.

Pork

A great deal of pork, *cerdo*, is eaten in Andalucía, mostly as hams and sausages. Indeed, these are such an important part of the Andaluz gastronomic landscape, that they get the next section of this book to themselves.

However, fresh pork makes a fairly frequent appearance on menus around the region, too – mostly as *lomo* (pork loin), though also as *chuletas* (chops), *costillas* (ribs), or *solomillo* (pork fillet).

Quail

Quail, or *codorniz*, is a wee bit smaller than a partridge and is farmed commercially. Purists may sniff that farmed birds aren't as flavoursome, but the rest of us can be grateful there aren't any bits of leadshot, guts or feathers to deal with before we get round to cooking them. By and large, recipes for quail and partridge are interchangeable, but you'll need less time to cook quail.

Rabbit

Most rabbit, *conejo*, is farmed too: and it's less flavoursome (though more tender) than the wild variety. You'll find it sold at the markets, generally at the *pollerías*, or poultry butchers. Popular rabbit offerings are *conejo al ajillo*, fried rabbit with garlic; and *arroz con conejo*, rabbit cooked with rice. *Gazapo* is baby rabbit, and this is frequently cooked *a la brasa*, grilled over hot coals.

In the La Espuela restaurant in Antequera they have developed a rabbit oil – *aceite de conejo*. This is a garlic and herb-flavoured olive oil, tasting mildly of rabbit, that they like to serve drizzled on their partridge paté. You can make it very simply: simmer a jointed rabbit in a litre of olive oil for about two hours, along with a head of garlic, a tablespoon of thyme, two bayleaves, a 20cm twig of rosemary, and 50ml of sherry vinegar. The rabbit can be eaten cold, and the strained oil will keep in the fridge for a month or so. Try it on salads.

Snails

Down here, everyone loves hunting for snails, or *caracoles*. After it has rained, people scoot out into the *campo* armed with a punctured bucket to collect the small brownish variety that are favoured right across Spain. Even the most committed of townies enjoy them: you'll find *caracoles* stalls in most of the main markets, with peasant farmers selling the creatures from sacks on the pavements, particularly in the springtime.

Snails are certainly popular as a snack. Spend a few minutes watching your fellow customers at a café, and you'll see them ordering glass tumblers full of the little molluscs, which they will dig out with a teaspoon and casually wrest from their shells.

If you are going to attempt cooking snails, do remember that they need a very thorough cleaning before they are edible. Usually this involves starving them for several days, or giving them flour to eat, which apparently purges them. Either way, the snails should then be washed well in several changes of cold water that's had salt or vinegar added. Put them in a pot of lukewarm water, bring slowly to the boil, and then simmer for at least an hour until tender. And you will need to put a good lid on the pot too, as the poor

critters will almost certainly try and make a dash for it. Snails are sometimes added to a sauce, but they are usually eaten on their own.

Venison

Venison, or *venado*, is either *ciervo* (red deer) or *corzo* (roe deer), and it's generally stewed. The same goes for wild boar, or *jabalí*. Both types of meat are popular as a chorizo in the sierras.

Charcuterie

It helps to like pork if you visit Andalucía: hams, sausages and charcuterie, collectively called *embutidos* or *chacinas* in Spanish, are one of the defining characteristics of the region's gastronomy.

You might suppose that with 800 years of Muslim rule in Andalucía, pork would have disappeared off the menu. But the enduring popularity stems at least partly from the great ease of rearing the animal: the pig doesn't need large green pastures or a specialist diet; indeed, it will cheerfully eat all your household waste, which makes it a jolly good recycling unit to have rootling outside the back door. And there's absolutely no waste with a butchered porker: everything, from tail to squeak, can be turned into a meal and eaten.

La matanza del cerdo is the traditional annual pig-killing, where a family and their neighbours will all pitch in together to slaughter the animal and transform it into various *embutidos*. The ritual is less common than it used to be, partly no doubt because of refrigeration, which means there is much less need to cure meat to keep it; and partly, of course, because keeping a pig tends to be slightly tricky in an apartment. But the numerous sausages, hams, and general piggy

bits and pieces that result are just as popular as they have always been.

Air drier

Andalucía produces some of the best air-dried ham in the world. It's called *jamón serrano* in Spanish, which literally means mountain ham, and this gives a small clue as to why it tastes so wonderful. The arid winds and cold winters of the sierras provide the ideal conditions to cure meat.

If you nibble on a paper-thin slither of *jamón*, experience the salt-sweet taste, and a texture that is lusciously sticky and chewy, you'll soon appreciate just why the Spanish take this ham so seriously. In fact, there isn't just one type of *jamón serrano*: there's a great variety, depending on the breed of the pig, how and where it has been reared, and what it has been eating.

If this all begins to sound a bit complicated, well, it isn't really because on the whole you get what you pay for. A top-of-the-range *jamón* will be expensive. And top-of-the-range out here means *jamón ibérico*, the ham made from the Ibérico pig, which is, as you'd imagine, a breed native to the Iberian peninsula.

Pigs In

The Ibérico pig has black trotters (and its ham is popularly referred to as *pata negra*, although this is misleading since there are several other breeds with black hooves); it also has long slender legs, a short neck, floppy ears and a pointy snout. But what makes the breed really special is that somewhere in its evolution there appears to have been a genetic development whereby fat, instead of being stored just under the skin, also began to filter into the muscles of the animal – making the meat much more succulent and flavoursome. Bear this in mind, when you come to choose your ham: make sure the meat has a marbled, flecked appearance rather than a uniform coral-brown colour.

And if you've ever wondered why all those ham legs hanging in the tapas bars have little conical paper cups dangling underneath them, it's because, thanks to the pigs' diet, the fat does genuinely start to ooze at room temperature.

At the absolute peak of the top-of-the-range hams, there's *jamón de bellota,* which is produced from Ibérico pigs that have roamed through the *dehesa* – oak woodlands – foraging exclusively on acorns for the last six months of their life. During this time, the pigs will have rootled their way through about eight kilos of acorns a day and put on around 70 kilos in weight. It's this combination of acorns and exercise that gives the ham its unique texture.

There is, moreover, a limit to the number of pigs who can experience this full acorn diet, partly because there is only so much woodland available, but also because the lucky ones need to be about a year old at the beginning of the autumn acorn season. Any poor porkers born outside this window of free-range opportunity will have to make do with grain. Their *jamón de recebo* still tastes exceptionally good, but it just isn't quite the same quality; and consequently, it's a bit cheaper.

Jamón ibérico is never used in cooking, except for the bone, which may be used to make stock. Ordinary *serrano* ham, on the other hand, being cheaper, is used in small quantities in countless recipes. One example is the delicious tapa, *habas con jamón,* where fresh broad beans are stewed in olive oil with spring onions and diced ham.

Incidentally, the leg is not the only joint that gets turned into *jamón.* The shoulder, or *paleta,* is also used. It has a higher bone-to-muscle ratio, though, and is therefore a cheaper proposition.

Ham on the range

Hams are produced all over Andalucía, but three areas are particularly well-known. First is the Sierra de Aracena region of Huelva province – where Jabugo is the village mostly closely associated with the *ibérico* hams, which have their own Denomination of Origin. Second is El Valle de los Pedroches in the province of Córdoba – here the White pig has been successfully and productively crossed with the Ibérico. And third is Trevelez – the main village amongst several in the Alpujarras south of Granada that produce hams from White pigs, for whom there is now a Specific Denomination of Origin, a classification that is on the way to being a DO. Trevelez is the highest of the villages in the mountain range, and myth has it that the hams from here are cured in snow. They're not, in fact, but it can get pretty parky in winter, and those icy breezes do make it an ideal situation for drying hams.

Sausages

Chorizo is easily the most popular type of sausage in Spain. It is available either *fresco* (raw) or *curado* (cured). The softer raw versions are used for cooking, and are often small sausages in a string, *en ristra.* They are frequently added to dishes like tripe, chickpea or lentil stews along with *morcilla* (see below), or eaten fried for a quick meal, accompanied by fried fresh peppers or a fried egg. They can also be cooked *a la plancha* (griddled) or *a la brasa* (cooked over hot coals) and served with bread as a tapa. Cured chorizo is generally eaten sliced, often as a tapa.

Chorizo is made with finely diced or minced pork and pork fat, garlic and *pimentón* (paprika), and sometimes with other seasonings, such as oregano. Chorizo can be *picante* (hot and spicy) or *dulce* (mild). There

Hamming it up

Slicing a leg of ham is a cross between an art form and a competitive sport: there are even national competitions to find the best carver. The sign of a good ham well carved? Well, arrange the slithers in a single layer on a plate, and then turn the whole lot upside down. The ham should stay put, thanks to a combination of the thinness of its carving and the richness of its fat. Needless to say, this is not something to try when there's an expectant dog underfoot.

To carve a ham properly, you need a special ham-stand called a *jamonero* to clamp it horizontally in place. An impressive selection of exotic knives is helpful too: at the very least, you'll need a broad-bladed one to strip the skin off; a pointy one to navigate around the bone; and a thin flexible long-bladed one to carve with.

Unlike other joints of meat, a ham is carved along the length of its muscle, and the aim is produce very thin slices of uniform thickness, with an outer edge of fat. You should only cut what you are going to eat, and it's good form to cover the ham with its skin, plus some greaseproof paper for good measure, to keep the meat moist.

Pig farm in Sierra Norte

is some variation in fattiness, too: if it's described as *más magro*, it will have more lean meat in it.

Hand-made chorizos may look different from one another, even when they've come from the same producer. There are several reasons for this. First, the colour of the *pimentón* ingredient may well vary; second, brighter conditions may have stopped the meat turning quite so red; and third, it may just be a question of time: chorizo slowly fades in colour as it ages.

Morcón is a type of chorizo, which is sometimes made from *cerdo ibérico*. The ingredients are placed in a fat piece of intestine, giving it its unusual round shape. *Masa de chorizo* or *picado de chorizo* is a more unusual way of eating chorizo. Rather than stuffing the ingredients into a casing, the mixture is shaped into small balls or flattened into burgers and then fried. And it's delicious. You can buy ready-to-cook *masa* in butcher's shops, or you may come across it as a hot tapa.

Longaniza is a loop of long thin fresh sausage (though you can buy it cured), which contains pork and pork fat, along with black pepper and cumin or cinnamon. It is used and eaten in much the same way as chorizo.

Chistorra is a long thin red-coloured fresh pork sausage (though sometimes it has a little beef added), which is similar to chorizo except that it is rather mild and garlicky. It originally came from Navarre, but is now a popular tapa everywhere.

Salchichón refers to any cured white sausage, similar to salami, with garlic and peppercorns added to the meat mix, and ready to eat without cooking. The white colour is down to the absence of paprika.

Morcilla is similar to British black pudding. It's a sausage containing pig's blood and pork fat, and is popular all over Spain; the *morcilla* from the north is particularly well regarded. Recipes for *morcilla* vary widely, though. It may include lots of onion and garlic – and spices such as cumin, cinnamon, paprika, clove, oregano and pine nuts are among the more unusual additions. It's generally prepared by being boiled and then dried, but it is always cooked again before eating. You'll find it used in a wide variety of meat and vegetable stews, or paired with tripe or pulses, often to bulk the dish out and give it extra flavour. It can also be griddled *a la plancha*, and trendy chefs occasionally like to caramelise *morcilla* cubes and serve little spoons of the mixture with foie gras. *Morcilla blanca* is rather similar to a *salchichón*, but it has saffron, eggs and garlic mixed in with the pork meat. It's especially popular in Córdoba and Jaén provinces.

Other pork products

Caña de lomo or *lomo embuchado* looks like a sausage because it comes in a skin, but actually it is solid meat: pork loin, in fact, marinaded in spices, garlic and wine. It is eaten sliced.

Lomo en manteca is fried and seasoned pork loin, preserved in lard. The meat is usually heated before eating, to melt away some of the lard – though true fans insist that bread dipped in it is one of life's great treats. *Lomo de orza* or *lomo en adobo* are similar to *lomo en manteca,* but the pork loin is preserved in olive oil.

Tocino is solid fibrous pork fat, cured in salt. A piece of *tocino* always goes into a *cocido* (the Andaluz one-pot dish of meat, chickpeas and vegetables) to add flavour and body.

Panceta is streaky bacon, smoked, or cured in salt. It is frequently served up as a tapa, griddled *a la plancha*.

Chicharrones are small pieces of pork meat – the cuts can vary from pork loin or pork scratchings to pigs' liver – mixed with lard and seasoned with garlic, salt, pepper, oregano, vinegar and paprika. They make a hearty breakfast spread on bread or toast.

Zurrapa is similar to *chicharrones,* but without the addition of paprika.

Sobrasada is a sausage made with minced pork, pork fat and paprika. It is best on a chilly night, grilled over an open fire and eaten with heaps of country bread. Originally from Mallorca, it's now also produced in Andalucía – although it doesn't have its own DO here as it does in Mallorca.

Fish

Fish, *pescado*, is caught all the way along the coastline of Andalucía, and towns throughout the region – even those nowhere near the sea – will all have a decent fish section in the municipal market. But if you are keen to find absolutely top-quality fish, then the markets to head for are in Cádiz and Huelva provinces, which have easy access to the Atlantic as well as the Mediterranean.

One Huelva good fish market

It has to be said, the city of Huelva is not at the top of most people's must-see list of places to visit in Spain, with one guide book even describing it as the least attractive and least interesting city in Andalucía. But pescophiles, don't let that deter you. The fish section at the market is the best ever: better even than Jerez and Sanlucár, and they are fantastic.

You've got to arrive early, though, and certainly no later than 9.30, to appreciate the full variety on offer. There are around seventy small fish stalls, all heaped high with spanking fresh fish and seafood. What's available depends on the season and the weather, of course, but you'll find tuna, swordfish, sole, over five different types of bream, red mullet, sea bass, whiting, hake, skate, mackerel, anchovies, sardines and turbot. And that's just the fish.

For Huelva is also famous for its love of *choco* (cuttlefish), so much so, that people from the city are affectionately known as *choqueros*. In the market there are even several stalls that only sell cuttlefish – a testament to its extraordinary popularity.

As for shellfish, you'll find quite a few different types of clam, including the *coquina*, a small wedge-shelled clam collected along the local

coastline where they abound. Among the crustaceans, there are normally several species of crab, and quite a few kinds of prawns, including Dublin Bay prawns and the famous *gamba blanca de Huelva*, the white prawn of Huelva – more on this one later.

If you can't make it to Huelva, you'll find most of the species listed below for sale at your market.

Anchovies, *boquerones*
These fish are ideal for frying, which is a good thing because in Andalucía cooks have turned fish-frying into an art form. The best anchovies are caught between Estepona and Nerja on the Costa del Sol, so in the markets there you'll be getting really fresh fish. The back should be a greenish colour: if it's gone black, then it was landed more than a couple of hours ago. Sometimes you'll come across anchovies served in *panojas* – five fish joined

at the tails in a fan shape. You should also try the tapa *boquerones en vinagre*. The headed and gutted fish is marinaded in vinegar and salt for a few hours, rinsed, and then covered with generous amounts of olive oil, chopped parsley and garlic. And if you happen to find yourself there, the local speciality in the Motril area of Granada province is dried anchovies.

Baby eels, *angulas*
Gone are the days when you could eat these with a clear conscience (pollution and popularity have combined disastrously and caused a dramatic slump in eel populations), so thank goodness the Japanese have shown the Spanish how to produce imitation ones, which you can buy in tins. They taste almost exactly the same – the only way you can tell the difference is that the tinned ones don't have eyes, and the manufacturers aren't allowed to call them angulas (though the brand names are designed to be very similar). Unlike crabsticks, those other fake fishy things, these are really rather good. You can serve them fried briefly in oodles of olive oil and fistfuls of slivered garlic, or piled into avocado halves.

Bonito, *bonito*
In terms of taste, this is a cross between a tuna and a mackerel. Bonito belly, *ventresca*, is the fattest and also the most delicate part of the fish. The best time to choose bonito is in the summer. It isn't quite as highly rated as tuna, and it is considerably cheaper.

Bream, Blue-spotted, *urta*
This is a fish that is common in the Bay of Cádiz. It is highly prized for its sweet-tasting flesh, which is the result of its shellfish diet. *Urta* caught off the coast of Rota in particular are considered the best, because there are large numbers, and a great variety, of

crustaceans found in these waters. And Rota is certainly the place to be in August when the town celebrates its annual *Fiesta de la Urta*.

Bream, Gilt-head, *dorada*
The *dorada* is easy to recognize, with a golden (or gilt) half-moon shape between its eyes. As with other members of the bream family, a favourite way of preparing this fish on the coast is stewing with peppers. Another method is to bake the fish whole in salt. So it's jolly helpful if you happen to have salt flats just down the road, as is the case in Cádiz province, as a one-kilo fish will need about the same weight of salt to encrust it adequately.

Bream, Red, *besugo*
This fish is traditionally served on Christmas Eve. Larger specimens often get baked, but it's also good chargrilled. You can distinguish the red bream from the others by its pinkish grey body and the large black spot behind the jaw. Other bream you may come across are Sea Bream, *pargo*, also called Red Porgy; and Pandora, or *breca*. Do try to choose the largest fish you can afford, even if this means sharing it, as these will have had more chance to breed. Fishermen are more than happy to use their precious quotas on catching high-value, plumper, bigger fish.

Chanquette, *chanquete*
Once upon a time, little chanquettes used to be found in the waters around Málaga and served up deep-fried in the manner of whitebait, but they were badly over-fished. Consequently other species started to be sold as chanquettes, which only made matters worse as, alas, they weren't this special small species at all, but just baby fish of various sorts. Eating these, frankly, is a bit like cutting the leg off a table and expecting it to remain stable: many fish are now

fighting extinction, and anything called chanquettes down here should definitely be off your menu.

Dogfish, *cazón*
Several small sharks are called dogfish; usually, the *cazón* is the nurse-hound shark, a close relative of the true dogfish, although people can be a little hazy about this. Anyhow, they taste pretty much the same, and I'm happy to opt for familiarity ahead of zoological accuracy this time. The fish is particularly popular in Cádiz, by the way.

Grouper, *mero*
Excellent grouper are found in the waters around Almería. In this province they like to serve grilled steaks with an orange sauce.

Hake, merluza
Hake is as popular and as ubiquitous on Spanish supper plates as cod is in British fish and chip shops. Always try to buy line-caught hake if you can, as the quality is far superior to those caught in trawler nets (also, the nets damage the seabed, and many other species get caught in them accidentally too). *Pijotas* are also common in the region: these are in fact small hake, served fried with their tails in their mouths.

Red Mullet, *salmonete*
The Romans did love their red mullet. And their favourite kind of garum, or fish sauce, was also made from red mullet livers. The

ruins of Baelo Claudia, where the Romans once made the stuff, is at Bolonia, just west of Tarifa. And to this day, the fish is still often cooked and eaten ungutted. Mind you, these days, the red mullet catch tends to be full of tiny specimens only fit for the stew pot, but if you do come across a large fish, then the best way to appreciate the great flavour of the flesh is to grill it.

Salt-cod, *bacalao*
Gerald Brenan in his book 'South from Granada' memorably describes the smell of

salt-cod as reminiscent of the lion house in a zoo. This hasn't stopped it from being very popular right across the region, though, despite the abundance of fresh fish. Significantly perhaps, bacalao was a permitted food on fast days, and it was once cheap enough to be regarded as the poor man's meat – even the most rural shop had a supply. Nowadays, however, the real McCoy is fairly expensive.

Salt-cod needs soaking before it can be used. Fillets called desmigado are common; these have already been boned and skinned, but they'll need a 24 hour soaking, with the water being changed several times. A thick whole piece of bacalao will need even longer. Alternatively you can buy ready-desalinated pieces from delicatessens.

Sardines, *sardinas*
Can there be anything more lip-smackingly

Great hake
A good way to cook hake fillets is to sprinkle them with lemon and salt, and put to one side while you liquidise 200g fresh peeled prawns with 100ml of dry sherry and 500ml of hot fish stock. Heat some oil in a frying-pan large enough to take the fillets in one layer, brown them on both sides for a minute, and then add the prawn sauce. Let everything bubble gently for three or four minutes more, and, if the sauce needs thickening, stir in some breadcrumbs.

Sole, *lenguado*

This is a wonderful fish, whose delicate flavour is sadly often submerged in sauce. It's actually best cooked *a la plancha*, or even fried. Look out, too, for the small species called *acedias*, that have a quite superb flavour.

Trout, *trucha*

The town of El Bosque in Cádiz province is famous for the trout that are caught in the local river, *el Majaceite*. Fly fishermen and women take note: this is the most southerly trout river in Europe. The local way of preparing the fish is with a slice or two of ham placed in the cavity before cooking – a method, incidentally, that is also common in the north of Spain. In Jaén province, though, which also has trout in its sierra streams, the most popular way of cooking it is *en escabeche*.

Tuna, *atún*

The coastline between Cadiz and Tarifa is much less developed than the Costa del Sol. It still has a strong fishing tradition and, more than anything else, is known for its seasonal capture of blue-fin tuna, using an ancestral method known as the *almadraba*.

How does this work? Well, a system of nets is used to corral the tuna into an area where there's a net resting on the seabed. This is then pulled up so that the tuna are left with very little water. The surrounding fishermen waiting in their boats then catch the fish with harpoons.

This ritual tuna-kill takes place every year between April and early June, when these fish migrate to their spawning grounds in the Mediterranean. Those that are caught, often weighing up to 300 kilos, are known as *atún*

delicious than the smoky-crisped skin and moist flesh of a spanking fresh sardine cooked over a fire, devoured to the sound of the ocean, and washed down with copious quantities of chilled white wine? To be perfectly honest, no – as the Andalucians know: they even have a name for this kind of midsummer, beachside, starlit fish-fest: *moraga*.

The way to cook sardines at an event like this is with *espetos*: sharpened pieces of split cane onto which the (ungutted) fish are speared. A fire is made on the leeward side of a bank of sand, and once it's burned down to the white-hot embers, the espetos are stabbed into the sand in a tepee formation so that the heat can cook the fish. Lemon is not usually squeezed over sardines, but you might find it useful for your fingers once you've finished eating.

Sea Bass, *lubina*

Sea bass is farmed throughout the Mediterranean. If you see a fishmonger's slab full of bass that are all the same size, then it's a fair enough bet that they're from a fish farm. The texture isn't quite as good, but you have to say that the flavour is fine. Sea bass is a great all-rounder: it can be grilled or poached with equal success. Try it served with a not-too-garlicky green gazpacho.

Skate, *raya*

This should really have a whiff of ammonia before you cook it – and don't worry, the smell disappears with cooking – as a wee bit of decomposition helps to develop the flavour. Skate is a cartilaginous fish, so those wings aren't full of bones at all, and in Spain you'll see the whole fish displayed, as bits from the tail and cheeks are prized as well.

de derecho. The meat is very red, firm and juicy and as a consequence, it is very highly prized – and not just by the Spanish. A large quantity of the best tuna is now bought by the Japanese whose large freezer ships instantly whisk the fish off to Japan to be served up as sushi.

When the tuna return to the Atlantic from their breeding grounds (starting in July and continuing until October) their meat is much leaner and drier, so it not so highly valued. These late season tuna are known as *atún de vuelta*.

Although meat is used from all parts of the fish, local chefs most highly prize the *ventresca* and the *morro*, from the belly and the fleshy part of the neck respectively. These cuts have a high oil content and, when cooked, result in meltingly succulent meat.

Tuna, dried, *mojama*
The process of turning fresh tuna into the salted dried version called *mojama* was introduced by the Phoenicians, who taught the local tribes how to make the most of the salt pans on their doorstep, and of the tuna in their coastal waters. And the same salt fields are still used today, although the bulldozer is now the preferred method for harvesting.

The fish are filleted and generously coated in salt crystals for two days before being thoroughly washed in running water and tied onto wire clamps for air-drying. This used to take place on rooftops to take advantage of the westerly breeze. Nowadays, the tuna is hung in large cold-storage rooms and blasted with air at a constant 14°C. After three weeks in these drying rooms, the mojama will have lost half its weight, and turned a deep muddy-red. The taste is highly concentrated and a little goes a very long way. Andalucians love *mojama* as a tapa, thinly sliced, like serrano ham, served on *bruschetta* with a drizzle of oil and some chopped tomato. You could also try tiny amounts of coarsely grated *mojama* scattered over *ajo blanco*, or even over home-made pizza, for that extra added oomph.

Super tuna
A typical tuna recipe from the area that is not only easy to cook but also totally delicious is tuna with onion, *atún encebollado*. Gently fry two finely sliced onions, a bayleaf and six black peppercorns in a generous amount of olive oil. When the mixture starts to turn golden, add about a kilo of tuna cut into three-centimetre chunks, season with salt, and sauté for another five minutes before adding a glass of fino sherry and simmering on a low heat for few minutes more. This is perfect with salad, and chunks of bread to mop up the juices.

Frying tonight
It's the familiar complaint – oh, it's only fried fish. But as anyone who has tried this method of cooking will tell you, it's not always that easy to do successfully. Here are the rules for frying fish the Andalucian way:

- Use a deep, wide, heavy frying-pan, filled almost two-thirds full with a mix of olive and sunflower oil.
- Heat the oil until it is very hot, about 170°C: it should be shimmering, but not smoking.
- Fish pieces should be small, and salted before frying.
- In Andalucía the fish is often coated with special fish-frying flour available in supermarkets. This flour is slightly coarser than ordinary cake flour – try maize flour if you're attempting it outside Spain.
- Don't cook too many pieces at once – the temperature will drop, your fish will end up oily, and your coating will go horribly soggy.

Málaga cooks are famous for their fish-frying talents, so try *fritura malagueña* – mixed fried fish – when you visit the city.

Shellfish

Here's a selection of shellfish, *mariscos,* commonly found in Andalucía:

Clams, *almejas*

Almejas is the generic term for bivalves; the best-flavoured species of clam is the little wedge-shelled *coquina* that you can eat raw. Small clams are known as *chirlas*.

Crab, *buey de mar*

The claws or *bocas* of the ordinary large crab (rather than the spider crab with its long spindly legs) are thought to resemble cattle horns, and that's why the Spanish call this crab the sea-ox. It's a popular tapa, and you'll see mounds of claws ready for sale in all the fish markets.

Mussels, *mejillones*

Mussels are a good-news story: they are easy to farm and the techniques involved don't damage the environment.
The floating rafts are an especially common sight in Galicia, with the cooler seas of the north providing better growing conditions than the polluted Mediterranean. Date-shell, or *dátil de mar*, is a long, thin mussel that is very good in soups.

Sea Urchin, *erizo de mar*

Beloved of trendy chefs everywhere, this mollusc is routinely turned into exquisite foams and mousses, but in truth it is probably best eaten raw with a squeeze of lemon. Pick one off the rocks when the moon is full, they say, because that is when the roes (the part that you eat) are at their plumpest.

Prawns, *gambas*

The *gamba blanca de Huelva*, the famous white prawn of Huelva, is considered by gastronomes to be the best in Spain, with a particularly wonderful and subtle flavour that is reflected in the price: on occasions they can sell for over €100 a kilo.

There's a degree of flexibility with the various names of prawns, as always. For example, shrimp fritters are often made with small prawns called *camarones*; true shrimps are *quisquillas*, and are also very popular. If you want to make fritters in the UK, by the way, use the little brown shrimps, the sort that are normally potted with clarified butter, mace and cayenne. *Carabineros* are also popular – see page 124 for a recipe.

To grill prawns, choose smallish ones and be prepared to pay a bit more for the tastier varieties. Brush them with oil, don't put oil in the pan, but do sprinkle a good pinch of salt in first. Cook in batches, allowing four to six prawns per person depending on size and greed, until they turn from grey to pink with a golden patina. Serve with lemon juice.

Cephalopods

Again, here's a selection:

Cuttlefish, *sepia*

Cuttlefish can be uncommonly good in the right hands, but on the whole, squid and octopus – to which cuttlefish are often compared – have the better flavour and texture. The people of Huelva, of course, will

disagree. They prepare cuttlefish, which they call *choco*, in just a thousand different ways; cooked whole, cut into strips and deep-fried, added into stews ... and they also love the roe. *Chipirones*, which are often called baby cuttlefish, are in fact a different species. They are delicious deep-fried, which is how you will usually come across them in restaurants. Just to confuse the issue, though, small squid are sometimes called *chipirones* too. But as they're on the danger list in terms of population collapse at the moment, you probably won't find them on the menu anyway.

Octopus, *pulpo*

Octopus is a popular tapa everywhere in Spain. Perhaps the passion for this creature reaches its zenith in Galicia, where *pulpeiras*, octopus sellers, are common, travelling round the fairs and festivals with their cauldrons or *caldeiras* of boiling octopi. Once cooked, the creatures are chopped up and dressed with olive oil and pimentón – both sweet and hot versions – and this must surely be the best way to eat them: *a la Gallega*.

Squid, *calamares*

Fresh squid are much more expensive than previously frozen ones, and much tastier too. I think they are best served very briefly grilled or fried, to take advantage of the lovely tender flesh. But frozen squid don't take to being cooked quickly like this, so just use them in stews. A good recipe from Almería combines squid with mushrooms, white wine, black pepper and saffron, with egg yolks used to thicken the sauce.

Vegetables

The Arabs not only introduced new vegetables to Andalucía, such as the aubergine and the cauliflower, but they were also responsible for a great deal of agricultural innovation, setting up highly effective irrigation systems for their new crops, and building hillside terraces which can still be seen today around the region.

Many of the fruits and vegetables that we all take for granted at home today were originally brought to Andalucía from the New World by Christopher Columbus: peppers, chillis, potatoes, tomatoes, pumpkins and avocados. Nonetheless, Andaluz cuisine still goes big on carbohydrates, with pulses and potatoes forming the bulk of the veggie side of things, and leaves and fruits mainly contributing the complementary flavours in their dishes. There are exceptions, of course: spring vegetables, such as asparagus and

artichokes, are always given a starring role when they're in season.

Here's a run-down of what to look for in the vegetable markets.

Artichoke, *alcachofa*
The artichoke, as you may know, is actually a flower, and spring is the best time to buy small the little artichoke buds, even though they are actually available all year round. The advantage of these babies is that the hairy choke has yet to develop, so preparing them is ultra-simple: boil gently until nearly soft, then simmer in wine in a cazuela; or split them down the middle, season and fry. By a happy chance of nature, baby artichokes are in season at the same time as baby broad beans: combining these two vegetables in a stew has been a traditional Mediterranean spring dish for centuries. And if you should happen to see artichokes labelled *alcaucil* or

alcarcil, then definitely snap them up, because these are a variety of wild artichoke that are especially flavoursome.

Asparagus, *esparrago*
You'll encounter two types of asparagus within the region: cultivated green asparagus (the crop grown around Huétor-Tájar in the province of Granada even has a Denominación de Origen); and *trigueros*, the thin stems of wild asparagus or sprue, which have a slightly more bitter flavour than the fat cultivated ones. White asparagus, which is produced by preventing the shoots from being exposed to sunshine, is a crop more typical of northern Spain. Asparagus is popular as a soup, and it also finds its way into tortilla, a Spanish-style omelette, as well as *revuelto*, glorified (and usually glorious) scrambled eggs. Always choose asparagus with firm unblemished stalks and tightly closed tips.

Aubergine, *berenjena*

The traditional Jewish way of preparing aubergines still persists today in Andalucía: slices are dipped in batter or beaten egg and then deep-fried – this is a delicious tapa. But the aubergine is also used in numerous other dishes, including *pisto*, the Spanish equivalent of ratatouille.

Broad beans, *habas*

Broad beans are used both fresh and dried. They combine beautifully with other vegetables, and with meat: *habas con jamón*, broad beans with air-dried ham, is one of the best-known Andalucian bean dishes; while *habas con choco*, broad beans and cuttlefish, is a speciality of Huelva.

Cucumber, *pepino*

The variety of cucumber you buy in Spain is fairly small, tough-skinned and actually rather tasty. It has been grown in the region since

Roman times, though it probably originated in southern India.

Garlic, *ajo*

Garlic was also very popular with the Romans, who used it extensively in their cuisine. Today, it is one of the most common ingredients in all the recipes of the region. Some will require a *cabeza de ajos*, a whole head of garlic, others a *diente* (clove) or two; garlic is often bought plaited into long strings called *ristras*. *Ajetes* or *ajos tiernos*, fresh green garlic shoots, are also eaten – usually in a *revuelto*.

Green beans, *judías verdes*

Judías verdes con jamón is a delicious tapa: steam the beans first, slice up some garlic, fry gently in olive oil, add the beans, stew for 10 minutes or so, and then add some diced ham, cooking this for just a few minutes – otherwise it'll turn to leather.

Lentils, *lentejas*

The lentils down here are the brownish green sort, not the split orange variety, and the most common way of using them is in a stew. Lentil stew is generally a fairly basic affair with just onions, peppers and garlic, but sometimes it will also feature chorizo and morcilla, or little bits of ham.

Mushrooms, *fungi*

By contrast to northern Spain, mushrooms have never featured very heavily in Andaluz cooking. But this is now gradually changing, with so-called wild mushrooms starting to appear on the better vegetable market stalls, and at supermarkets such as El Corte Inglés. There have always been pockets of traditional enthusiasts, though, in the mountainous regions, and nowhere more so than at the Parque Natural Sierra de Aracena y Picos de Aroche. More than 700 types of fungi or mushrooms have been identified in this area, and around forty edible varieties are enjoyed by the locals.

Onion, *cebolla*

Onions are the bedrock of all Spanish savoury dishes. Spanish onions have a high sugar content and therefore caramelise deliciously. Some Andaluz recipes will specify *cebolleta*, also known as *cebolla tierna* – this is a large salad onion with a mild flavour.

Pepper, *pimiento*

The pepper was another import from the New World, and more often than not in Andalucía it gets fried. A delightful vegetarian version of *calamares* is a speciality of the Huelvan fishing town of El Rompido: this is *calamares del campo*, or squid from the countryside. Actually, it's deep-fried peppers, but it's a vegetarian nibble that even the most vehement meat eater will enjoy. Fried green *padrón* peppers, occasionally very hot ones, are an import from northern Spain that is catching on down south too. The *choricero* peppers, that you see hanging up in long strings, generally end up diced and added to soups, stews, and casseroles.

Potato, *patata*

The Spanish were the first people to use the potato as a food in Europe. It arrived in Andalucía in the 1550s from Colombia, where the Spanish expeditionary forces had described the tuber as a "truffle of good flavour". It wasn't, by any means, an instant hit, though. The early potatoes tasted rather bitter, and had a watery texture that didn't compare well to other new discoveries such as the sweet potato and the Jerusalem artichoke. Indeed, it wasn't until 1573, when a Seville hospital decided to try them on its patients (at knockdown prices) and were pleased with the nutritious results, that potato cultivation slowly began to catch on in Andalucía – with poor people and soldiers generally being the main consumers. For this reason, potatoes tend to appear mainly in traditional peasant meals, like *patatas a lo pobre*, in which potatoes are gently softened in olive oil along with another new world vegetable, green pepper. But as well as featuring in casseroles and one-pot dishes, potatoes are also a key ingredient in some salads, such as *ensalada Malagueña*, a combination with salt-cod, orange, onion and olives.

Pulses, *legumbres*

Pulses are central to everyday eating in Andalucía, as they are in the rest of Spain. Various lentils and beans, *alubias* and *judias*, are available dried, and also ready-to-use in jars. The *habichuela*, a variety of dried white bean, makes a frequent appearance on the

Cocidos: meals in a pot

A *cocido* is a one-pot meal, something of a cross between a soup and a stew, made up of meat, vegetables and chickpeas. There are almost as many variations on the recipe as there are cooks in the region, since the whole thing depends entirely on what ingredients happen to be available. But your average cocido might include a cut of beef, a pork rib or some ham bones, a slice of pork fat, a bit of chorizo and some morcilla, along with potatoes, green beans, onion, a full head of garlic, some swiss chard, and plenty of chickpeas (soaked overnight). Once cooked – and these days, the pressure cooker is the favoured way of speeding up all the simmering that's involved – the cocido is eaten as two courses. First, the chickpeas, vegetables and stock are served as a soup, and then for the second course the meats are placed on a big platter in the middle of the table, and everyone helps themselves, slicing off pieces and chopping them all together into a mixture they call *pringá*. The traditional accompaniment is bread.

The most common variation on cocido is *puchero*. The ingredients are more or less the same, though the veggies tend to be potatoes, carrots, leeks and celery – and chicken legs seem to feature quite often, too. Perhaps the main difference is one of intent: the busy working parent will set out to make this stew last a good few days, by ensuring that the leftovers can be used up in any one of several different ways.

Whatever goes into the pot, a key objective will always be the generation of plenty of stock, because, once meal number one – veggies and pringá – has been scoffed, the stock will be used as the basis for at least a couple more meals. One favourite is to use it as a basis for a soup, *sopa de puchero*, into which chopped-up hard-boiled egg, chopped serrano ham and mint, and occasionally little pieces of fried bread are typically added. Alternatively, the cook might use it in a soupy vegetable *arroz* (rice dish), or baste it over roast meat – rabbit or chicken, for example. Meanwhile, any leftover meat from the puchero is traditionally used to make croquettes, called – unsurprisingly enough – *croquetas de puchero*. And if the family aren't driven to mutiny at having to eat up their Sunday lunch yet again, then those leftover chickpeas are often turned into a salad, with tomato and onion, along with either tuna or egg.

Andalucian table – it's also, incidentally, the name of a famous flamenco singer from Granada: Juan Habichuela. But perhaps the most commonly used pulse is the chickpea, or *garbanzo*. Chickpeas with salt-cod is a very typical tapa, as is chickpeas with spinach, which is particularly popular in Seville. But more often than not, chickpeas turn up in a *cocido* – the name given to an almost infinite variety of local stews.

Pumpkin, *calabaza*
Pumpkin is one of those veggies that lurk in the background, being used a lot but rarely lauded. You'll come across it stewed or fried, and it's a common addition to the region's many *cocido* dishes. Pumpkins, along with large courgettes and marrows, will also appear in some versions of *pisto*.

Spinach, *espinaca*
Spinach and swiss chard, *acelgas*, may be used interchangeably. Both collapse when cooked, even though chard looks and feels more robust. Spinach and chard are usually added to bean stews, and they may also be cooked with other vegetables like carrots and leeks, before being puréed and served as a side dish.

Tomato, *tomate*
The tomato, whose name is derived from the Aztec *tomatl*, has always inspired suspicion: when it was first introduced, people thought it was poisonous. And even today not everyone appreciates its world domination. Juan Carlos Alonso, a food writer from Seville, reckons the tomato, along with the pepper, has had an overall negative influence on cooking, as it's too easy to add tomato to dishes to give them flavour. Consequently, he maintains, Andaluz cooking is less subtle and refined than it was centuries ago. His is a minority position, though: for better or worse, tomatoes are now an integral part of the regional cuisine. Convents and monasteries were early enthusiasts: there's a splendidly-titled manuscript dating from the mid-seventeenth century, *el libro de la cocinacion de los capuchinos de la provincia de Andalucía,* which has several tomato-based recipes. And from these obscure beginnings, the tomato has now risen to take a starring role in the kitchen. Most famously, tomatoes are one of the three main ingredients in the traditional Andaluz *gazpacho* and its relatives, *salmorejo* and *porra*.

Herbs and spices

Flick through any Andalucian cookery book and you will come across frequent references to *majado*. This is a mix of herbs and spices, frequently also containing garlic and almonds, which is added to Andaluz dishes such as *cocido* or *espinacas con garbanzos*, and is frequently used to thicken the sauces of stews and casseroles. The term comes from *majar*, meaning to pound or grind, and refers to the way that seasonings and other ingredients are traditionally crushed together before being added to a dish. In the past this would have been done with a pestle (*mano*) and mortar (*mortero*), but these days it's more likely to be done with an electric handheld blender.

Marinades, such as *adobo* and *escabeche*, are also common here, and in fact have their origin in the Moorish cuisine of Andalucía. Before the era of refrigeration, the marinade was a standard way of keeping fish fresh: an *adobo* is still used for those fish that don't have a great deal of natural flavour – for example, *cazón*, a type of shark, or *boquerones*, which are fresh anchovies. The traditional ingredients are vinegar, salt, garlic, paprika, cumin and oregano. *Escabeche* (from the Arabic *iskabay*) is another common vinegar-based marinade, traditionally used for sardines and also, oddly, for partridge.

Spices are used more in Andalucía than in other parts of Spain, but even so, the cooking of the region is not overtly spicy: the aim is generally just to provide background flavour. Spices and herbs can be bought loose in markets or specialist food shops, but you should look for a stall with a high turnover, to guarantee quality and flavour.

Here are the herbs and spices you will most commonly encounter as you explore Andalucía's markets and restaurants:

Herbs

Bayleaf, *laurel*
Bayleaves make an appearance in stews, casseroles, marinades and rice dishes. They can be bought, fresh or dry, in big bunches from the market. Dried leaves are particularly useful for marinades, whose recipes often stipulate that the bayleaf should be crumbled.

Coriander, *cilantro*
Green coriander is especially popular in Portugal, and consequently you will find it used most frequently in neighbouring Huelva province, and less commonly in the rest of Andalucía. It does pop up from time to time in gazpacho recipes, though.

Fennel, *hinojo*
The feathery leaves of the cultivated bulb fennel are really rather insipid when compared to the hot aniseed intensity of its wild cousin, which grows in abundance everywhere. *Puchero de hinojos* is a fabulous soupy vegetable stew common in springtime before the fennel herb goes to seed. The leaves are combined fresh and dried with beans and potatoes, along with a ham bone to boost up the flavour.

Mint, *hierbabuena*
No *sopa de picadillo* (see page 117) would be complete without a few small leaves of mint floating in it. But this herb is also the standard last-minute addition to a *caldo* – the local broth made with chicken stock, a beef bone, carrot, leek or onion, and potato. This is traditionally drunk from a mug or cup rather

than eaten from a bowl, and if you are cold, ill, or just the worse for wear after too much booze, then you will immediately be given a mug of minted *caldo* before being packed off to bed. Carmen Ladrón, who owns La Cartuja de Cazalla, a converted Carthusian monastery, reports that the monks, who couldn't have this soup because their order was vegetarian, originally bred terrapins, *galapagos*, in their pool to provide themselves with a tasty meat-free stock.

Oregano, *oregano*
Dried oregano is frequently used in meat dishes and marinades. It also crops up in black puddings and in *chicharrones*, which are a tasty mix of pork fat and pieces of pork commonly eaten spread on bread or toast for breakfast.

Parsley, *perejil*
The most popular herb in Andalucian cookery, this is used – fresh – in fish, soup,

and meatball recipes, as well as in casseroles and stewed dishes. If you are buying fruit and vegetables from a market stall and you also ask for parsley, they will frequently give you a bunch for free.

Rosemary, *romero*
Rosemary grows wild and in abundance across the region, although curiously it isn't much used in cooking. But you'll find it occasionally perking up a soupy rice dish, and it has also become popular as a coating for goat's cheese.

Thyme, *tomillo*
Fresh sprigs of this herb are tucked under roast lamb, game and fish dishes, and added to marinades such as those used for olives. Several varieties of thyme such as *T.almoradux* grow wild in the sierras, where some country folk still like to forage for their culinary requirements.

Spices

Chilli, *guindilla*
Red chillis can be bought whole, or ground up as cayenne, *cayena*. This is not used a great deal in Andaluz cuisine, and when it does make an appearance, it's generally in rather timorous quantities, in snail and meat dishes.

Cinnamon, *canela*
Cinnamon came across with the Arabs, and is commonly used in sweet dishes like rice pudding, custard pudding and *bienmesabe*, a dessert with almonds, sponge cake and angel's-hair pumpkin jam. It is also found dusted on top of traditional confections made by nuns, as well as making an appearance in certain meat and offal dishes. It can be bought in sticks or ready-ground.

Cumin, *comino*
Yes, this spice came over with the Arabs too,

and is used mainly in meat and fish dishes, as ground cumin (*una pizca de comino*: a pinch of cumin) or sometimes as whole seeds, or *cominos*. No *pincho moruno* (Moorish kebab) would taste right without cumin; nor would *morcilla* (black pudding).

Paprika, *pimentón*
This is made from smoked and ground-up sweet peppers, which were originally introduced into Spain from South America following the Spanish conquest. There are three types of pimentón: *dulce*, which is mild and smoky; *agridulce*, which has a stronger flavour and a sharp aftertaste; and *picante*, which is appreciably hotter. Paprika is sold in tins and generally keeps its flavour fairly well. It is used extensively in all kinds of dishes, including chorizo, black pudding and other sausages.

Saffron, *azafrán*
Saffron is made from the dark orange-coloured stigmas of the October-flowering *crocus sativus* (which isn't your common-or-garden variety, so don't bother with DIY saffron!). The name comes from Arabic *zafaran*, which means yellow. The saffron crocus originates from Iran, but has been cultivated in Spain since 960 AD, mostly in La Mancha, although some is also grown in Andalucía. It's a highly labour-intensive spice to produce: the stigmas can only be picked by hand, and one hectare of flowers yields only about nine kilos of dried saffron. In other words, real saffron is extremely expensive, and it's fortunate that very little is needed to perfume and colour a dish. In fact, a generous pinch is not at all a good thing, as the flavour is rather bitter when it's overused. Saffron is normally sold in delicately-matted crinkly threads, *en hebra*. When you want to add some to your cooking, you first dry out the threads in a small frying-pan over a gentle heat, and then grind them with a pestle and mortar – you'll find they turn to powder very easily. Saffron is frequently used in Andaluz cuisine: in rice, fish and shellfish dishes, as well as in meat, chickpea and vegetable casseroles.

You will also find, occasionally, cloves, sesame seeds, anise, and whole black peppercorns used in the local cooking.

A walk on the wild side
When times have been hard, Andalucians have always gone out into the countryside to forage for food. And these days, despite being better off, they still head off into the *campo* to collect certain foods – either because some things are only available growing wild, or just for the fun of it.

Colleja, bladder campion, is traditionally collected in the spring and is often added to a *tortilla*, Spanish omelette; it's said to taste much like young spinach. And the stems of the *tagarnina* (a low-growing golden thistle) are often added to a *revuelto* dish of scrambled eggs. There is even a word *tagardinero*, to refer to someone who collects and sells *tagarninas* to eke out a living.

Fruit
Most of Andalucía is mild and frost-free, which doesn't particularly suit the poor old apple tree, but does mean that some fairly exotic fruits can be grown in the region. The market gardens of the Costa Tropical in the province of Granada, for example, produce mangos, kiwis and passion fruit – and growers are experimenting with new crops all the time.

The notion of seasonality is well on the way to being dispensed with, in fact, not only on the Granada coastline but also in Almería, which keeps Spain and the rest of Europe supplied with fruit and veg all year round. It is a slightly surreal experience to drive through this arid desert-like countryside, with hectares and hectares of land all covered in a patchwork of tatty plastic poly-tunnels and greenhouses. Mind you, these horticultural shanty towns might not look very beautiful, but they have generated large amounts of wealth in an erstwhile impoverished area – as well as creating considerable concern about the environmental impact of this industrial agriculture on the underground water reserves.

These are the fruits to look out for in Andalucía:

Almonds, *almendras*
Almonds originated in the eastern Mediterranean, so it's no surprise that they are well adapted to the climate here: they don't need much water and they come equipped with deep roots to extract what little moisture there is. In early spring, head for the Axarquía region of Málaga, and the Lecrín valley, halfway between the city of Granada and the coast, to witness confetti groves of pinky white blossom.

The Arabs used almonds in both sweet and savoury dishes, and this habit persists today. The cold soup *ajo blanco* is made from ground almonds; and these are also used to thicken sauces, as well as being a principal ingredient in confections such as *queso de almendra* and convent cookies (see page 49). It makes a huge difference to these recipes, in terms of flavour, if you can find the time to grind the almonds yourself. Buy the whole ones with skins on, and scald the required amount with boiling water. You'll find they pop out of their skins very easily, and then it's simply a question of grinding them in a food processor.

One of the highlights of a visit to a Spanish supermarket, by the way, is the *frutos secos* counter where you can buy salted almonds by the kilo.

Apricot, *albaricoque*
Apricots don't appear in savoury dishes, or

even in desserts for that matter – which is slightly surprising, since on their journey from China they successfully managed to infiltrate the meat stews and rice dishes of Persia and Morocco. Here in Andalucía, though, they are eaten just as they are, or in the most delicious of jams, or drunk as a fruit juice.

Avocado, *aguacate*
The avocado came over originally from South America as the *pera de las Indias*, or Indian pear. The most common variety found locally is the Hass avocado – a small variety with a dark greeny-brown rough-textured skin and a deep yellow flesh.

Cherries, *cerezas*
The Romans loved cherries: the fruit was highly prized by emperors and ordinary citizens alike. Legend has it that the great Roman epicure Lucullus, who introduced the cherry into Europe in around 70 BC, killed

himself when he found he had only a few thousand of the fruit left. Although Andalucía has not so far been known as one of the great cherry-growing areas of Spain, cultivation is increasing here.

Chestnuts, *castañas*
You always know when autumn has arrived in Spain, as the vendors set up their braziers on street corners and sell roast chestnuts to passers-by. Hand-warming as well as belly-filling, chestnuts were traditionally given to the cathedral congregations keeping vigil for All Souls' Day (1 November).

Chestnuts are most commonly found in the Serranía de Ronda in Málaga province. In this area they are most popular in their dried form, and when they are available like this, they are called *pilongas*. Huelva is another province where chestnuts grow, in the Sierra de Aracena. The trees were introduced in

The Romans considered the fig tree to be sacred, and it became traditional to give these fruits as New Year presents; though presumably not fresh ones, as they ripen at the end of summer and go rotten pretty quickly. Drying them in the sun is a practical and fairly obvious solution to the problem – although the Moors simply squeezed out the juice and boiled it down into a syrup. Another wizard way, typical of the province of Málaga, is *pan de higos*: dried figs are chopped and mixed with almonds and spice – cinnamon and crushed cloves, for example. The mixture is then moulded into a flat cake and left for several weeks with something heavy on top of it, to compress the mixture. Try nibbling a small slice with a piece of strong cheese – it's delicious.

Grapes, *uvas*

Grapes have a long history in the region. Apart from their use in wine production, grapes were a favourite Roman way of finishing a meal. Alcohol is, of course, prohibited under Islam, but the cultivation of vines continued under Moorish rule, with the fruit being used to produce distillations for perfumes and medicines, as well as the raisins that still feature in so many Arab dishes.

A strategically placed vine or two in a backyard has always been useful source of shade as well as fresh grapes. Granada's Albaicín district is famous for its *carmenes*, which are houses set in walled gardens. The word *carmen* comes from an Arabic word, *karm*, meaning grapevine: traditionally these courtyards were kitchen gardens.

Málaga raisins, *pasas de Málaga*, have a *Denominación de Origen* label. They are wonderful, large, fat, sweet raisins made by drying Muscat grapes: the best ones are still

the fifteenth century (from Galicia, which has the biggest chestnut crop in Spain) but they are now starting to show their age: the crop is no longer as plentiful as it once was. Even so, they feature in many delicious local dishes such as *caldereta con castañas* – a ham, bean and chestnut hotpot. Chestnuts are the only nuts that you have to boil or roast before using, and it is quite a fiddle getting the skins off. The good news is that these days you can buy jars of ready-peeled nuts. Check out Sierra Rica (www.sierrarica.com), an Aracena-based company producing organic chestnuts, which you can find in many supermarkets, and which are also exported to the UK.

Chestnuts, incidentally, contain the same kind of carbohydrate as potatoes, and you can use them in similar ways. Carmen Ladrón de Guevara Bracho from La Cartuja de Cazalla in the Sierra Norte, for example,

recommends them mashed with a pot roast. Of course you can use chestnuts in sweet dishes too: look out for chestnut purée, chestnuts in brandy and chestnut cream.

Custard apple, *chirimoya*

The custard apple tree originally came from the subtropical zones of Peru and Colombia, and has been cultivated along the coast between Granada and Málaga since the sixteenth century: these days custard apples from the area actually have a Denominación de Origen label. These are odd-looking fruits, it has to be said, rather like round fat pears with a scaly green rind: they don't travel well, and they don't keep long either, as the skin is somewhat delicate. Try to avoid the seeds as you spoon into the creamy sweet flesh. The flesh discolours on contact with air, by the way, so don't make the mistake of thinking you might save some for later.

in a bunch when you buy them. They are produced in the Axarquía region, a mountainous region behind Málaga city, and in the towns of Manilva and Casares in the far west of the province. The grapes are harvested in whole bunches and laid outdoors in the sunshine on drying trellises or *paseros*, where they stay, slowly wrinkling, until December or January. Málaga raisins are delicious as a snack, as any child with a yellow mini-box will tell you, but they're also used in savoury dishes. And why not try using them instead of grapes or melon as an accompaniment to the cold almond soup *ajo blanco*? Incidentally, if you happen to be invited anywhere in Spain on New Year's Eve, it's traditional to eat a grape at every chime, for good luck.

Medlar, *níspero*

Medlars, or loquats, are in season between April and June, and fill a gap before the arrival of more interesting fruit such as peaches. They are an orange-coloured, smooth-skinned, slightly pear-shaped fruit, with juicy, rather tart flesh. Handle with care: they bruise easily.

Melon, *melón*

Along with watermelon, *sandía*, melons are a major fruit crop in Almería. They are the fruit of choice on *menus del dia* when they are in season between June and September.

Orange, *naranja*

Seville bitter oranges were first introduced here as ornamental trees. Anyone keen on garden design should head for the Patio de los Naranjos, by the side of the great mosque in Córdoba, as this is the oldest surviving example of how the Arabs used orange trees in gardens. Seville trees are much hardier, and therefore less prone to disease, than their sweet cousins, and so most Andalucian towns have bitter orange

trees lining the streets. Seville is the paradigm example, of course, and there are always visitors to this city who, on seeing trees laden with fruit, make the mistake of helping themselves. It is something of a local sport to watch their smiles turn into grimacing spits.

All the same, Seville oranges have made it into the kitchen: the sharp tangy juice is an essential ingredient in *caldillo de perro*, which literally means dog's broth, but is in fact a fish soup from Cádiz. And some versions of *gazpachuelo* and *cachorreñas*, both popular in Málaga province, stipulate a good squeeze of bitter orange.

But for the British, of course, Seville oranges mean only one thing: marmalade. This, along with sherry, is evidence of the long trading history that this area of Spain has had with Britain. The word marmalade comes from *marmelada*, actually Portuguese for a sweet,

solid quince paste that was exported to Britain in the late fifteenth century to be used for medicine. In Tudor times lemons and Seville oranges were made into preserves that were also called marmalades, although these were in fact solid confections that had to be cut with a knife, in much the same way as modern-day *membrillo*. By the nineteenth century, though, "real" marmalade was being produced and sent out to every corner of the British Empire. A tin of marmalade from Scott's ill-fated Antarctic expedition was discovered buried in the ice in 1980 – still, incidentally, in perfect condition. (In fact, Seville oranges have a very short season – in January – but they can be frozen, so remember to put a kilo or so in your freezer, and enjoy the juice in dishes all year round.)

Such was the importance of marmalade to Britain that during World War II a trade

agreement was struck with the Franco regime for the import of Seville oranges. The British government apparently deemed marmalade to be an integral part of the British diet, and absolutely essential for the maintenance of morale. The civilian shipping company who had the contract to transport the oranges, though, paid a heavy price, losing four ships: one was sabotaged at sea by a bomb hidden among the oranges – something to ponder as you bite into your breakfast toast.

Sweet oranges, brought down by Portuguese traders, arrived in the region about 400 years after the Seville oranges. These fruits are a principal ingredient in salads such as *remojón*, a combination of oranges, salt-cod and onion. And have you looked in the mirror lately and groaned at your jaded complexion? Then peel and chop an orange into rounds, arrange on a flat plate and dribble olive oil over the slices, followed by a sprinkling of

sugar – and commit to eating this on a daily basis. A glamorous and fast-living Marbella-based Englishwoman back in the 70s lived on a diet of this, along with copious quantities of champagne and the occasional bowl of lentil stew. Her skin was absolutely fantastic, admirers recall.

Peach, *melocotón*
Peaches originated in China, where references to their cultivation go back three thousand years. By 330 BC they had arrived in Greece via Persia, and they reached Europe in the Middle Ages. In Andalucía they are grown mostly in the provinces of Seville and Huelva, from where the first fruits come towards the end of May. They are in season from this time until about the end of September.

Persimmon, *caqui*
You won't see these in the markets until the autumn. Look out for trays of orange-red,

tomato-shaped fruit: the ones to choose are those with skins that are starting to split, a sure sign that the fruit is ripe. Eat them immediately: they won't keep. The pips are edible, but have a texture reminiscent of lumps of gelatine that have refused to melt.

Pomegranate, *granada*
The Romans had a curious use for pomegranate: they ate the seeds but tanned the thick skin to make a type of leather. The fruit was brought into Andalucía by the Arabs and from there it soon spread to the rest of Europe. Granada, of course, adopted the fruit as its symbol, and it now appears all over the city: on historic buildings, fountains, street-name plaques and on the ubiquitous blue and green glazed Granadine pottery. Pomegranate is not only eaten as a fruit in the region; the seeds also appear as an ingredient in some recipes – for example, in a local variation on the salt-cod and orange salad, *remojón*.

Prickly pear, *higo chumbo*
It was the Spanish *conquistadores* who first brought prickly pears back from the New World. The fruit, which ripen towards the end of summer, are either yellow-pink or red, and they have nasty spines: many of these look like fine hairs, but if you handle the unpeeled fruit you will certainly notice the effects for some days afterwards. Much better to leave the picking and peeling of chumbos to the experts: buy them ready-to-eat in shops, or from the gypsies who collect them in the countryside and then set up their stalls outside the main markets.

Quince, *membrillo*
The autumn-ripening quince looks a bit like an overweight lumpy pear; when ripe, it is the colour of October sunshine. The main quince-producing area in Andalucía is around Puente Genil in Córdoba province,

and many houses in the sierras will have a tree or two in their gardens. The flesh of the fruit is fairly dry and grainy, and it is quite sharp-flavoured too, so it needs to be cooked before eating; in Andalucía it is most frequently made into a preserve known as *dulce de membrillo*, or into *carne de membrillo* – quince jelly.

To make *membrillo*, wash, peel, core and cut up two quinces (about 600g). Cover with water and boil for about fifteen minutes until soft. Drain the quinces and pass them through a sieve. Add the same weight of sugar to the quince purée, mix well and return the mixture to the saucepan. Keep on a low flame for about an hour, stirring from time to time. Put into a rectangular mould and let the jelly set. Keep refrigerated. Membrillo is great diced into tiny pieces, and mixed into a salad of lettuce, olives and nuggets of hard nutty goat's cheese. Or try it

with blue cheese at the end of a meal, accompanied by a sweet oloroso.

Strawberry, *fresa*
The strawberry was an American immigrant, arriving in the nineteenth century from Virginia. Nowadays, around half of Europe's strawberries come from the province of Huelva in Andalucía. The agricultural land close to the coastline has become another poly-tunnel landscape, and the two towns most associated with strawberries are Palos de la Frontera and Lepe, the latter being by far the biggest producer. A large berry called the *fresón* is the favoured variety and, as anyone buying an out-of-season strawberry might have noticed, this is a large, heart-shaped, bright red fruit that is sadly lacking in the flavour department. The first Spanish strawberries make their appearance in local markets early in March, and continue to be available until about July.

Organic food

Spain is Europe's fourth-largest organic food producer. What's more, with olive oil accounting for 40% of sales, Andalucía is the top region in Spain for this approach to farming. With statistics like these, you might think it would be easy to find organic foodstuffs here, but actually this isn't the case, because Spain exports 99% of its "bío" produce.

In fact, organically-grown food for local consumption has taken quite a while to catch on – partly, I suspect, because this approach embodies what most farmers were doing a couple of generations ago, when they couldn't afford pesticides and fertilizers: it's precisely the kind of farming that many people always wanted to get away from. But, with the growth of the urban middle classes, and the realisation that shiny uniform oranges that last for weeks don't actually

taste that great, organics are now gradually becoming easier to find. Interest has also been fuelled by foreigners from northern Europe demanding what is now easily found in supermarkets in Germany and the UK. Consequently, there are growing numbers of small local producers around the region, many of whom work as co-operatives and supply through independent weekly markets. Also, the daily municipal markets often have stallholders who are selling local produce that isn't necessarily *labelled* organic, but which for all intents and purposes will be.

Markets and farm shops

Órgiva, a village in the Alpujarras, has a well-known organic weekly market. Any visitor will quickly become aware that the whole village is fairly "alternative", and Andy and Carol Trotman, who have a stall at the market, are a classic example of incomers dedicated to working the land organically.

Their biodynamic farming system was taught them by an elderly neighbour who had worked their plot of land for over fifty years, using the phases of the moon as a guide for planting and harvesting, and thereby continuing a tradition that even predates the Phoenicians. The Trotmans also run a barter scheme in which people can come and work on their farm for a day in exchange for a box of organic produce. Telephone 666 243 736 for more details.

Permaculturacañadulce is a *finca* (estate) with one and a half hectares of land on the bank of the Río Grande, 9 km from Coín, in Málaga. It had been left fallow for thirteen years and had never been subjected to any chemical treatment, so it was an ideal place for Matricia Lana and Lucho Iglesias to create a permaculture-based organic design from scratch. Reforesting was one of their first tasks, and there are now masses of fruit trees including oranges, mandarins, grapefruits, avocados, persimmons, loquats, peaches, apples, pears, figs, almonds, pecans, and olives – as well as a number of medicinal herbs. The finca also runs courses throughout the year in permaculture, vegetarian cooking and yoga (as well as Spanish for foreigners wanting something a bit different). Visit www.permaculturacanadulce.org for more information.

La Semilla, in Bolonia, near Tarifa, was established as an alternative to the dominant development model so common along the *costas*. The founders have returned the land to its natural state, reintroducing indigenous plants, in an eco-village that is designed to be self-sufficient. Their restaurant is vegetarian, with much of the food coming from their own garden, and with ingredients like tofu being hand-made in the kitchen. They also make their own bread which they sell locally. "We get people coming from all over," Chris told me. "It's a beautiful place to spend a day, as you can look around the site or just enjoy the stunning views from the terrace." La Semilla also hold regular courses and day workshops. For more information telephone 652 102 001 or visit www.lasemilla.ourproject.org

Farmers' Markets are still a new idea in Andalucía, although they're well established in the UK, for example, with a variety of small producers selling fruit, vegetables, home-made cakes and pies, alongside the work of artists and craftspeople. There are two main locations in Andalucía:

Fridays at Aguamania, Cartama, on the Coín road, at km 2, 11am – 3pm; and Tuesdays at Chiringuito Antonio, A335 Vélez Málaga – Alhama de Granada Road, at km 104, opposite the Periana turning; between 10am and 2pm.

Telephone 952 118 096 for more information.

Agrícola de los Pueblos Blancos' produce is worth looking out for: this is an organics-only co-operative that set up business in 2004. Farms belonging to the co-operative include La Verde, Cádiz province's first organic venture, growing over 35 different tomato varieties; El Bosco, which produces soft fruit, herbs and salad greens; and Antonio Mulero's farm near Prado del Rey where eleven varieties of plum are grown, along with peaches, apricots and quinces. Antonio is currently experimenting with organic greenhouses for his beans and tomatoes.

BioCórdoba is now in its tenth year and is an annual gathering of organic producers from around the region. It has developed from just a handful of stalls to nearly a hundred, showcasing everything from freshly picked fruits and vegetables to honeys and hams. While much of the produce goes for export, the aim of the fair is also to educate people locally. BioCórdoba takes place in mid-April (the dates will vary each year) at the Palacio de la Merced, Córdoba. You can get further information from www.epea.es (an organisation representing organic companies and producers in Andalucía).

Organic Shops
Bionatura, the original organic supermarket on the Costa del Sol, now has two branches: one in los Boliches, Fuengirola, and one in Marbella. Primarily driven by the health benefits of organic food, they began by catering to the many foreign residents in the Fuengirola area, especially those with health problems that required a non-toxic diet. Three years ago they opened a second shop in Marbella to cope with demand from

further down the coast, and both shops are now extremely popular, as organic produce (especially fresh fruit and vegetables) is still hard to find.
Av los Boliches 112, Edif Laura, Fuengirola
C Felix Rodríguez de la Fuente s/n, Marbella
Tel: 952 900 401

Tea Time is a *tetería* or tea shop; these are very popular in Andalucía. They are generally alcohol-free, and many are heavily influenced by Arabic traditions and decor, serving a range of teas accompanied by sweet pastries and snacks. Tea Time in Estepona may well stock the widest range of teas in Spain. Nearly 400 varieties line the shelves, and the choice is so bewildering that it's a good thing Birgit the German owner is on hand to advise. Many of the teas are organic, and she sells a range of organic essential oils as well.
Av Andalucía, Residencial La Viña II, local 2D, Estepona
Tel: 952 794 657
Web: www.universodehierbas.com

Camac wholefood shop is owned and run by Steve and Audrey Lee. They also run an organic farm nearby, and have a straightforward philosophy: "We like good quality food that hasn't been messed about with," says Audrey. "And we really enjoy helping people find their favourite wholefoods." The well-stocked shop has a good range of fresh and packaged foods, including many special items for those on wheat-free, dairy-free and diabetic diets. Organic fruit and vegetables are sourced locally wherever possible, which Steve says is "good for the environment and good for the local economy – and, because we know the suppliers, we know it's truly organic."
C Real 23 bajo, Órgiva, Las Alpujarras
Tel: 958 784 616

Not just sherry

The drinks cupboard

Wines

Glance around the next restaurant or bar you visit in Andalucía, and the chances are you'll see visitors drinking Rioja. Which is fine. But it's a bit like going to the Alsace region of France and choosing a bottle from Bordeaux: you're not exactly making the most of your opportunity to discover the vast range of great wines available locally.

Andalucía is where wine-making in Spain first began. Wherever there are a couple of rows of grapes there'll be someone making wine – even if EU regulations mean that much of this will be considered agricultural produce only, and therefore not allowed to be sold in bottles. (For an explanation of wine labelling regulations see the next page.)

Most villages in the wine-making areas will have a bodega (or even just a farmyard) where you can buy wine by the litre for a couple of euros. It goes without saying that this is plonk, for immediate consumption; but, more often than not, it's jolly good plonk.

There are currently five *Denominación de Origen* wine regions in Andalucía:
DO Jerez/Xéres/Sherry y Manzanilla
DO Montilla-Moriles
DO Málaga
DO Sierras de Málaga
DO Condado de Huelva

DO Jerez/Xéres/Sherry y Manzanilla

The region of production in this Denominación de Origen is popularly known as the "Sherry Triangle", formed by the towns of Jerez de la Frontera, El Puerto de Santa María and Sanlúcar de Barrameda.

Sherry, the fortified wine produced in this area, is not only unique to Andalucía: it is also famous worldwide. In practically every city in the world there will be at least one restaurant with a bottle of sherry on the drinks trolley. This isn't simply because the bodegas are brilliant at distribution; the fact is, if you fancy something with zing and subtlety, which goes brilliantly with food, then sherry is just a great choice of wine.

DO you know?

Once wine is inside a bottle, it is subject to three possible classifications:

Denominación de Origen is the top quality level, and refers to the territory in which a wine is produced. It is the result of the efforts made by the wine-makers of a particular area to produce an original wine that is specific to that defined territory. A regulatory council is set up to specify, implement and monitor all the rules and criteria that govern the DO in question. Some DOs are very stringent, and specify everything, from the limit on the yield of a vine, to the maximum number of shoots that can be left after pruning, or the percentage of grape varieties that are allowed in any blend – and that is before the wine is even made! Other DOs are more liberal, but even so they will have strict quality control as their raison d'être.

Vino de la Tierra is the second tier, the not-quite-DO-yet classification, if you like. Bottles may well carry the name of the area and the vintage date.

Vino de Mesa is the third class possible. This simply means table wine, and, under EU law, neither the year, nor the grape variety, nor even the geographic location, are allowed to appear on the label.

It's worth remembering that good wineries will often have mixture of DO and non-DO labelled wine, because wine-makers are a creative bunch who tend to chafe at such restrictions – which are, after all, a bit like demanding that a chef can only make lasagne according to one strictly defined recipe. As a result, you can quite easily find outstanding wines – most usually experimental reds – that nevertheless have to be classified as *Vino de Mesa*. Similarly, you may well find young *cosecha* wines from trendy experimental wine-makers commanding higher prices than wines that have been aged for longer.

And it is important to remember that sherry is wine, because if your only experience of it to date is a slurp from a half-empty dust-encrusted bottle retrieved from the back of the drinks cupboard, then it's not surprising that you thought it horrid. After all, how tempted would you expect to be, by a room-temperature white wine opened a couple of months previously?

Admittedly, if you are between forty and fifty-five, then you can be forgiven for being a bit sniffy about the stuff. You reached the legal drinking age at just about the time when the sherry industry had lost its way and gone downmarket. You can probably recall a sickly-sweet brown beverage called British Sherry (it doesn't exist any more) that was filling the fortified wine sections of UK supermarkets, just as we were all discovering the joys of great Chardonnay.

In fact, younger sherry devotees are often those who were fortunate enough to have parents who were regular sherry drinkers. These are the youngsters who didn't have to wait till they reached the legal drinking age: while Dad was out gardening, they'd sneak into the dining room (where all the decanters would be arranged) and help themselves to a swift swig of Croft Original – neat whisky being a little too demanding for their young palates.

Well, whichever is closest to your experience, the good news is that quality sherry never went away, and in fact it's now becoming widely available and appreciated once again. Even better – sherry is ridiculously good value. You can buy a light, elegant fino for the same price as a plonk that tastes like paint stripper.

Sherry grapes

There are many sherry styles, which we'll look at in a moment, but it may surprise you to know that there are only three main grape varieties used in sherry production.

Palomino grapes are used in 95% of all sherry production. It's one of the many contradictions of Andalucía that such a terrific drink as sherry should come from such an unpromising grape as this. For when the Palomino is grown for ordinary wines elsewhere, the results are, well, ordinary. This variety is, however, ideally suited to the chalky soils and prevailing winds of the area – conditions which result in large quantities of the perfect wine for turning into sherry.

Pedro Ximénez, commonly known as PX, is another white grape that is grown elsewhere in Andalucía and made into dry wines. In Jerez, however, this variety is turned into an almost-black sweet sherry – it is often then used to sweeten up the Palomino-based dry sherries, but it may also be bottled by itself. In fact, almost no PX is grown in the Jerez region at all: most of it is brought in from Montilla-Moriles and aged in Jerez – a rare instance in Spanish DO regulation where this sort of import is permitted.

Moscatel, or Muscat, is a grape variety used in the sherry region to produce high quality wines bearing the Moscatel name. The vines grow best in vineyards located close to the sea, and the resulting wines are grapey and floral to taste.

The sherry-making process

It's worth knowing a bit about how sherry is made, because it is the process, rather than the grapes, that lies behind all the marvellous tastes and styles of the wine.

Pressing

At harvest time in September, the Palomino grapes are whisked off to the wine-presses where they are very gently "traded", or tumbled, to break the skins and release the grape juice. The first light pressing will extract around 70 litres of "must" or *mosto de yema* from every 100 kg of grapes. And it's this first pressing that is used to make sherry. (The bodegas usually carry out a second and third pressing: the second will be used for sherry vinegar; the third is usually destined for the distillery.)

Fermenting

Just like ordinary table wine, the grape juice now ferments in large steel tanks for three months, to achieve 12 or 13% alcohol. By now, the all-important yeasts called *flor* are beginning to grow on the surface of the wines – these can be anything from a thin film to a thick foamy gunge. At this point, the tasters arrive, and it is their job to decide on the kind of ageing the wines are to undergo. The palest wines, clean and especially light, will be set aside for ageing *bajo flor,* or under the yeast cover: this type of ageing will produce the very light *fino* and *manzanilla* styles of sherry. Other wines, still clean on the nose and palate, but judged to have a bit more body about

Jerez

them, are destined to become the deeper *oloroso* styles.

Fortifying

Now the wines have their alcohol content increased – wines fortified like this are known as *generosos* – usually by the addition of grape alcohol. At this stage, the yeasty flor is fundamentally important. A fino sherry needs to have a vigorous growth of yeast on it: this thick layer will protect the wine from the air. Consequently, fino wines are fortified to 15.5% alcohol, which is the ideal strength for the flor to thrive: and this leads to "biological ageing" rather than "oxidative ageing", since the wine is not in contact with the air.

Wine that is to become oloroso, on the other hand, is fortified to 17.5%: at this strength, the yeast cover naturally dies off, and the wine then begins to undergo the oxidative ageing that will give it its more complex and aromatic character.

Ageing

Ageing is really the key part of the sherry-making process. All sherries must be aged for at least three years; but many sherry styles in fact depend on being aged for considerably longer than this.

Once fortified, the wines are transferred to 600-litre American oak barrels for the first stage of their ageing, which lasts about a year. Unlike other wines, which age in hermetically-sealed tanks or barrels to prevent oxidation, sherry butts are only filled to about three-quarters of their capacity, and air is allowed to come into the barrel, thanks to an unsealed hole at the top. In this way, the region's specific climatic conditions can now begin to play their part in the sherry-ageing process. Indeed, the difference between a fino and a manzanilla is simply that manzanilla wines are aged at Sanlucár, near the coast, where the extra humidity in the air allows the yeast cover to flourish all year round, resulting in an even paler, and slightly saltier, style of fino sherry.

The most important part of the sherry-ageing process, though, is the *solera* and *criadera* system, which involves gradual and fractional blending of the young wines with more mature wines, whose qualities they begin to acquire. It works like this: the rows of sherry barrels are stacked in layers. The solera is the bottom layer, the one at ground level, containing the oldest wines. As these wines become ready for bottling, the barrels are partially drawn off, and then topped up with wine from the row immediately above – the first *criadera*. And so the process goes on, with each layer being replenished with wine from the layer above, up to the top

row, where the barrels are topped up with relatively new wine.

The wine that is drawn from the solera is either bottled immediately, or used in a *cabeceo*, or blending. It is at this point, for example, that a dry oloroso might be blended with sweeter wines, to create medium and cream sherries.

Sherry vintages

All sherries were actually vintage wines until about 1800, but the continuous fractional blending of the solera system means that nowadays you can't really call a sherry a vintage: it's a blend of different wines from different years, more or less by definition.

However, in absolutely exceptional years, a bodega may decide to set some wine aside for separate ageing, and, if they don't decide to incorporate it later into the solera system,

then it may eventually appear as vintage sherry – rare stuff, of course, and correspondingly expensive.

It has to be said, though, that some of the great sherries, vintage or no vintage, contain some very mature and venerable wine indeed.

Sherry ages

In recognition of this, in July 2000, an age-dated sherry category was introduced. This classification has to be approved by the Consejo Regulador, and, since calculating the average age of a sherry solera is pretty difficult, their main criterion is that the sherry must exhibit the *characteristics* of wine of a certain age.

• VORS (Vinum Optimum Rare Signatum, or Very Old Rare Sherry) is a sherry of at least 30 years of age, though some

examples may in fact be considerably older than this.
• VOS (Vinum Optimum Signatum, or Very Old Sherry) is a sherry of at least 20 years of age.
• Two further categories – for 15-year-old and 12-year-old sherries – have since been added, and these came onto the market in 2004.

It is certainly a complicated process to get a wine labelled with these terms. A wine-maker who wants to bottle a sherry as VOS or VORS will have to extract the wine from the butts and transfer it into a stainless vat or similar container. Someone from the Consejo Regulador will then come along to take samples: the quantity of wine in the container will be noted, and the vat will be sealed. The samples will then need to be approved by a tasting panel as being of sufficient quality to merit VOS or VORS status. If, and only if, this test is passed, then the average age of the wine is calculated, often using carbon-dating methods. And only then will the producer be given the requisite number of labels for the quantity of wine that was sealed in the vat.

Bodega architecture

It's worth remembering that the bodegas themselves, as buildings, play a crucial role in the development of sherry. They are always impressive and occasionally beautiful, but most importantly they are supremely functional.

This region of Spain, after all, enjoys some 300 days of sun each year. And there are two prevailing winds: the *levante*, which is the tail-end of the sirocco, is a hot dry wind that blows in from the south-east; the *poniente*, by contrast, comes in from the south and west, and is a fresh moist breeze that will aerate and refresh the bodegas.

Jerez wine-growers have adapted to these conditions by building their cellars in such a way as to ensure minimum sun and maximum cool humid breeze. Windows are set high up in the walls, to prevent sunlight from falling onto the butts, and are covered with grass blinds that allow sea breezes to enter while keeping out the light.

Bodegas are often located close to the sea or on relatively high airy sites, so that the wines in the barrels can benefit from the coolness of the morning sea breezes and the westerly winds. The floors are laid with sand, lime and iron oxide, which are sprinkled with water twice a week in summer in order to keep the cellars cool.

And, oh, the smell! Wander through the cellars for any length of time and you'll become quite heady with the gorgeous, sharp, yeasty, winey scent that permeates these marvellous buildings.

Sherry styles

No other style of wine has quite such a rainbow of tastes, aromas and colours as sherry. The different types of ageing – biological, oxidative, or a combination of both – mean that a wine can gradually take on any one of an immense variety of hues, ranging from a very pale straw yellow to something that looks as though it could tar roads. And the blending of sweet wines with dry wines adds yet another variable.

Fino, as we have mentioned, is the lightest and driest of the sherries. It is a wine that should be drunk young, so don't keep a bottle thinking it will improve with age. And make sure you buy your sherry from a shop or bodega that has a high throughput, to ensure it is as fresh as possible. The top-

selling brands include the excellent Tío Pepe (from González Byass), La Ina (Allied Domecq), and Tío Mateo (Márques del Real Tesoro). There are plenty of really good finos, but the best of all has to be Valdespino's Ynocente.

Manzanilla is a fino, as we have seen, but one that has been matured (though not necessarily grown) in the Sanlúcar area of the Jerez DO. The higher humidity here means that the yeast *flor* tends to maintain a thick covering on the wine all year round, and that in turn results in a slightly different flavour: the sherry is less aromatic, but has an almost salty tang. These differences are pretty subtle: some finos may seem to you to taste more like manzanillas, and vice versa. My advice is: when in Sanlúcar drink plenty of manzanilla, and don't get too hung up on the terminology – just memorise the label if you like it. One of the biggest

brands is La Guita from Hijos de Rainer Pérez Marin: this was the first manzanilla to have its bottling date on the back label. There are two versions: white label and yellow label – the yellow is aged slightly longer, and travels better. Really aged manzanilla is called *manzanilla pasada*: this wine stays in the solera for between eight and fifteen years.

Amontillado starts off as a fino, but remains much longer in the system. After about eight years, a fino will start to oxidise and take on the amontillado characteristics of a darker colour and a more robust aroma – while still managing to retain the tangy taste of the fino it once was. Excellent examples include Amontillado del Duque (González Byass), or Reserva Los Arcos (Emilio Lustau). And if you want to try something really special, try Bodegas Tradición's Amontillado VORS.

Harvey's Bristol Cream and Croft Original. Other good examples include Emilio Lustau's East India Solera and Sandeman's Character Medium-Dry. Unfortunately, quite a few creams are fabricated by simply mixing in fructose or grape concentrate. Pale Cream sherry, incidentally, is a sweetened fino.

Medium sherries are sweetened olorosos, and in the old days used to be called *Amorosos*. It's rather a shame they aren't still – I suspect we'd all be more tempted to say yes if offered some amoroso on a chilly evening.

Moscatel is made with sun-dried grapes. It is often used to sweeten other sherries, but you can also find it as an unblended wine, with a grapey, rather floral taste.

Incidentally, it is actually possible to produce an amontillado without fortification, by ageing a fino for longer than normal, until the yeast dies off due to lack of nutrients. The raising of the alcohol level, to 17 or 18%, is then brought about by slow evaporation. The Fino Imperial produced by Paternina is an example of this process.

Oloroso means fragrant in Spanish, and that is exactly what this style of sherry is: aromatic and complex, both to taste and smell. There is also a lovely softness to it, due to the tiny amount of glycerine present from the ageing process. It's a style that encourages thoughtful sipping, rather than carefree swigging. Good examples include Matusalem from González Byass, Fernando de Castilla's Antique Oloroso, and Oloroso de Jerez Ángel Zamorano – an *Almacenista* sherry from Emilio Lustau (see below).

Palo Cortado is a happy quirk of nature: it starts life as a fino, with all that lovely flor, and then it throws a sort of vinous wobbly, loses the flor, and launches itself into an oxidative ageing process. Experts describe palo cortado as having the nose of an amontillado and the taste of an oloroso. The rest of us are just grateful that such a delicious sherry exists. Actually, amontillado is sometimes blended commercially with oloroso, but it's not the same thing. Real palo cortado is rare and expensive. One of the best is the 60-year-old Sibarita from Domecq. Or try and get hold of Palo Cortado Viejo from Hidalgo.

Cream sherries are definitely blends: all sherries start off as dry, but by adding PX sherry and then returning the mix to the solera, some very good sherries indeed can be created. Best-selling cream brands are

Pedro Ximénez, PX for short, is dark, sweet and intense: you sometimes come across wine experts describing it as having flavours of liquorice, or chocolate, or burnt coffee, or even tinned tomatoes with sardines. Take no notice. Try PX Napoleon by Vinicola Hidalgo, or El Candado Valdespino and Manuel de Argueso PX.

Sherry Do's And Don'ts

- Do serve fino and manzanilla chilled.
- Do drink up – or buy half a bottle if you only want a small quantity.
- Don't keep open fino and manzanilla in the fridge longer than three days.
- Don't keep any sherry, no matter how sweet, for months.
- Do use a tulip-shaped white wine glass – no need to buy a set of copitas until you're a fully-fledged sherry anorak.

Sherry with food

Fino and **manzanilla** should be served well-chilled, and are ideal aperitifs. But they are also great accompaniments to a meal, whether it be with soup, seafood, white fish or mild cheese. Certainly both are drunk with tapas as a matter of course in Andalucía.

Amontillado is delicious on its own, but also goes well with light soups and consommés, white meats, blue fish and meat terrines. Amontillado should be served cool, rather than cold.

Palo cortado and **dry oloroso** are complex-tasting wines, for rich foods. They should partner cheeses, roasted or smoked venison, and game. They can also stand up to such difficult-to-match foods as eggs, artichokes and asparagus. These wines should be served slightly cooled.

Cream and **medium** sherries, along with **sweet oloroso,** are marvellous partners for desserts – fruit-based ones, in particular. But do experiment and try them also with foie gras and other kinds of patés; and they can be wonderful with membrillo and cheese. These wines should be served slightly chilled if the day is warm, but at room temperature if the weather is cool.

Pedro Ximénez can be partnered with foods in a similar way to cream sherries, but remember that this style is even sweeter. It is perfect poured over ice cream, in fact, or served with other rich puddings, especially chocolatey ones.

Moscatel is an ideal wine to serve with all types of pastries, and with blue cheeses.

Sherry in cooking

"Bad soup needs sherry; good soup deserves it," an aged great-aunt once observed to me, as she poured a generous amount into her steaming bowl. A crafty way of getting herself a bit more booze, or a great culinary tip? Certainly there is a place for sherry in cooking. It is, after all, essential in trifle, one of the glories of British cooking (if it's home-made); and it makes Madeira cake taste wonderful, too. PX can also be used to deglaze the juices from roast pork, resulting in a sublime gravy. Meanwhile, a generous glass of fino or manzanilla is even better than white wine when added to shellfish such as clams: pour it in just as the shells are about to open. By all means, do experiment by substituting sherries in cooking for both white and red wines, but do also bear in mind how they are used in Andaluz recipes – they can make a dish taste quite different. The nuttier-tasting sherries are very good in offal dishes, for example. Check out the recipe section for more ideas.

Sherry bodegas to visit

The best way to try, and to buy, sherry is to visit the region and its bodegas. You can of course buy sherry throughout Andalucía, but you won't really get to experience the full range unless you go where it's made. Anyway, the towns are charming, and each bodega is unique – which is a great excuse to visit several. Here's a selection of those that are highly recommended:

Jerez

Bodegas Pilar Aranda is named after the first woman to become a master of sherry, and it's been going since 1730 – which is in fact what their main label is called. The range isn't big, but the sherries in it are all very good: amontillado, palo cortado, oloroso, and PX. And if you should happen upon a bottle of their VORS Alburejo Oloroso, buy it immediately, because it's perfectly delicious.

They are also well-known for their excellent sherry vinegar, which consequently is difficult to get hold of – though Seville airport sometimes has a stock. In addition, they take their brandy, Duque de Veragua, pretty seriously too: Swarovski – of crystal fame – have designed a bottle for them.

Álvaro Domecq, who found he missed the sherry business when his family sold out to Allied Lyons, bought the bodega in 1998. He was also a *rejoneador*, a bullfighter on horseback, and then, when he got too old for that, he became a leading bull breeder. There are plenty of reminders of these interests in the bodega, with mounted bulls' heads everywhere.

Visits by prior arrangement
Tel: 956 339 634
Address: C Alamos 23
Web: alvarodomecq.com

Bodegas Tradición is unique: the only bodega in Jerez to concentrate solely on the production of VOS and VORS wines. They select sherry from a wide selection of other bodegas, and then put them into their own soleras. The result is a small but exceptional range of sherries, such as:

Amontillado VORS, classified as 37 years old. The solera uses sherry from the nineteenth-century Alfred Gilbey bodega, that has long since ceased to exist, along with others from Bobadilla, Osborne, and Delgado-Zuleta.

Oloroso VORS, classified as 39 years old. This wine comes from blending Domecq soleras from the eighteenth century with Alfred Gilbey's soleras from the nineteenth century.

Palo Cortado VORS, classified as 32 years old. The solera blends sherry from eighteenth-century Domecq soleras with

Croft harvests from 1970 and 1982. **Pedro Ximénez VOS**, classified as 20 years old, which mixes Sandeman soleras from the nineteenth century with Harvey's sherry.

None of these is cheap, but then neither is decent malt whisky – and sherry like this is well worthy of the comparison. You can spend a good half-hour with a glass from any of these four sherries, just marvelling at the complexity of taste and smell: magical and mysterious.

And the enterprise really is a labour of love, established by three men from great sherry-making dynasties: Ignacio López de Carrizosa Domecq, Javier Domecq and Joaquín Rivero Valcarce. The bodega itself is a tiny, charming renovated nineteenth-century building in the heart of the old walled quarter of Jerez. It features a collection of antique oil paintings; several tiles drawn by Picasso (aged eight!) are also embedded in one of the walls.

Visits by appointment
Tel: 956 168 628
Address: Plaza Cordobeses 3
Web: www.bodegastradicion.com

Emilio Lustau is an elegant and innovative bodega producing serious sherry, as you will already know if you're a sherry enthusiast. Those of you who have yet to be converted should make a point of visiting and trying the wines. Their Puerto Fino is fantastic, and regularly wins awards.

But what really sets this bodega apart is its Almacenista range. *Almacenista* means stockholder, and here in Jerez it refers to someone who buys sherry or grape juice from farmers in the area and then ages it in his or her own bodega. Almacenistas are not allowed to bottle their own sherries, however, and in the past these were sold on to larger commercial sherry houses; but Lustau recognised that some of them were already wonderful and didn't need blending with anything else. They now showcase and promote these Almacenistas under their own brand umbrella. As you would expect, though, they are produced in small quantities and can be difficult to get hold of. Still, help is at hand. The Emilio Lustau Sherry Club has been established to promote global interest in Almacenista sherries, and there are now 6,500 members worldwide. The club is free to join, and offers its members various benefits such as subsidised annual trips to Jerez; lunches, dinners and special events; tastings; and the opportunity to buy specialist sherries.

Visits by appointment
Tel: 956 341 597
Address: C Arcos 53
Web: www.emilio-lustau.com

Sanlúcar de Barrameda

Fernando de Castilla produces a stylishly-packaged range of sherries, brandies and vinegars, whose contents are better even than their upmarket branding suggests. The chic little bodega is located in the centre of Jerez and the driving force behind it is Jan Pettersen, a Norwegian, who decided on a career involving Spain, sunshine and sherry while doing his military service on the Russian border up in the Arctic Circle. He took over the bodega after working for fifteen years with the Osborne Group, who are headquartered down the road in Puerto del Santa María.

He is as passionate about the immaculate restoration of his buildings as he is about the quality of his wines – which are bottled in the most natural state possible, with no blending, and no cold treatments or stabilization techniques, thus ensuring that all their subtle aromas and tastes are retained. The same

principle is used for his brandies and his sherry vinegar.

Accolades have come in from The Wine Society, who extolled the PX as one of the best they'd tasted, and from Wine International, who gave the Antique Oloroso a 96 out of a 100 score.

However, it is brandy that Fernando de Castilla is best-known for. Using a distillate produced especially for them in La Mancha, and old-fashioned wood-burning pot stills, the brandy goes through the solera system process, being aged in barrels that have previously contained old oloroso and amontillado sherry. The result is a really gorgeous silky brandy.

The bodega has also managed to keep its old-fashioned charm: Charlie the cat will probably accompany you as you tour around

the place. Right next door is a *tabanco* (C Jardinillo 16), a combined shop and bar where you can buy sherry by the glass or jug or indeed whatever container you have to hand. Drop in around mid-morning and you'll find elderly gentlemen here knocking back sherry and putting the world to rights. This kind of place is often called a *despacho de vino* and is generally more common in Sanlúcar de Barrameda.

Tours by appointment only
Tel: 956 182 454
Address: C Jardinillo 7 al 11
Web: www.fernandodecastilla.com

González-Byass manages the difficult feat of being a family-owned business that produces quality wines which are exported globally. Tío Pepe, one of its main brands, is not only produced in vast quantities (it is Spain's best-selling sherry); it also manages to be one of the best finos on the market.

A visit to their bodega is a must-do, especially for anyone with a Disney bent, as they even have resident dipsomaniac mice who have a little step-ladder left for them to climb, to allow them to sip from a glass of PX. But this is only one small part of the experience for the 100,000 visitors a year who pass through the architecturally varied and historically interesting bodegas. There is also a very good bar and shop for anyone who wants to bypass the entertainment and get straight down to experimenting.

As you might expect, they produce a wide range of sherries. Besides Tío Pepe, examples of their everyday wines include Croft Original, and their manzanilla, called El Rocío, which is excellent. Serious sherry aficionados are also well catered for. The Apostoles are 13 huge oak barrels, each one named after an apostle, and containing sherry from very old soleras; a small quantity of palo cortado is released as Apostoles sherry every year. The thirteenth barrel, Judas, contains vinegar, as the company also produces a range of these – including a sweet PX that makes a worthy alternative to balsamic vinegar. There are also seven different brandies to discover, all of which are excellent.

Tours: Monday to Saturday, mornings and afternoons; Sunday, mornings only
Tel: 956 357 000
Address: C Manuel María González 12
Web: www.gonzalezbyass.com

Márques del Real Tesoro & Valdespino

Valdespino, owned by Grupo Estévez, is a huge, newly-built bodega on the outskirts of Jerez – but don't let that put you off. Not only does it produce a great range of sherries, but there is also a lot to see, thanks to the wide interests of chairman José Estévez (you'll recognise him by the labrador who is his constant companion).

For starters, the main reception has an extraordinary collection of antique grandfather clocks and writing bureaux. Then, over in the visitor centre, there is a permanent art exhibition displaying works by Picasso, Dalí, Miró and other Spanish artists. Horse fans will also be interested by the stables, dedicated to the breeding of Andalucian horses, and the carriage museum, which includes a tack room with traditional harnesses and saddles. These are all still used as part of the celebrations in the spring *feria*.

And even if you have already seen several bodegas, do still have a look around the soleras – which will be literally music to your ears, as they are currently experimenting with harmonious sound, to see if this will improve the quality of the sherry as it ages.

The Real Tesoro brand covers ten different sherries, including Tío Mateo Fino and Del Príncipe Amontillado. But the jewel in the crown for Estévez is their Valdespino bodega, which they bought in 1999. Valdespino's premium fino is the award-winning Ynocente, which is without doubt one of the best on the market. The grapes come from only one vineyard, the best in the area, and the must is still fermented in oak barrels, not stainless steel tanks. What's more, ten criaderas are used, rather than the more usual two or three, giving the fino greater depth and complexity. Other Valdespino wines to try include Amontillado Tío Diego and VOS Oloroso 1842, which have both won major awards in the last three years.

Visits by arrangement
Tel: 956 321 004
Address: Ctra Nacional IV km 640
Web: www.grupoestevez.com

El Maestro Sierra is special, not just because it produces outstanding sherry, but also because it is owned and run by women. It started life as an Almacenista, producing sherries which it sold on in barrels to other sherry houses, and was later bought by master cooper José Antonio Sierra. A couple of generations later, in 1976, Pilar Pla took over the running of the business, and in 1992 she decided to market sherries under the bodega's own label. Pilar is now in her eighties and still brims with charm and charisma; her personality is reflected in the bodega's quality wines. Unusually, they produce an *amoroso*, a beautifully-named sherry that also tastes quite divine. And do try their Palo Cortado and Oloroso Extra Viejo; in fact, try them all.

Visits by appointment, Monday to Friday, 10am to 2pm
Tel: 956 342 433
Address: Plaza de Silos 5
Web: www.maestrosierra.com

El Puerto de Santa María

Osborne is a very English name for a Spanish bodega, but that is because the wine trader Thomas Osborne Mann from Exeter settled in Cádiz 200 years ago, and several generations later his business is still owned by the family, and indeed is now a global drinks company. Located in the attractive town of Puerto del Santa María, the visitor centre is an attractive bodega reminiscent of an English colonial clubhouse, with lovely courtyard gardens full of exotic plants, and comfy leather chairs to sit in while you taste the sherry.

The company is probably best-known for its brandies, but it also produces some very good sherries: Fino Quinta, Bailén Oloroso, Coquinero Amontillado and PX Viejo are all brands to look out for.

Jerez

Tours in English are available, Monday to Friday, starting at 10.30am
Tel: 956 869 000
Address: C Fernán Caballero 3, El Puerto de Santa María
Web: www.osborne.es

Sanlúcar de Barrameda

Sanlúcar is famous for its seaside horse racing, but for foodies there's an even better reason to visit this town earlier in the year, for every May there is a very popular manzanilla fiesta. And where there's a chilled glass of manzanilla, there's usually some scrumptious shellfish to go with it, making it a very jolly few days of celebration. Not all of the bodegas are open to the public, but here's a few that are.

Barbadillo are one of the biggest wine-makers in town, and they make a great manzanilla called Solear. Their Oloroso Seco Cuco is also very well regarded. The bodega

A bull market

Osborne is famous for its black bull silhouette billboard – see the front cover of this book – that has transcended advertising to become an official historic monument.

Back in 1956, the bull was designed as an advert for the company's Veterano brandy; in those days it was a mere four metres high and made of wood. But three years later the bull had developed into a sheet metal design, with Osborne Sherry and Brandy emblazoned across it, and stood about ten metres taller than its earlier cousin. It remained in

this form for a further 25 years, until there was suddenly a ban on roadside advertising.

The public response to the ban, though, was rather like a bull sitting on a bee. A massive Save the Bull campaign sprang up, lasting several years, with everybody from the Department of Culture to journalists and film stars joining in. The rumpus was all finally worth it, as the Supreme Court eventually decided in the bull's favour, declaring it to be part of the local landscape. Consequently the ninety-odd giant bulls that were then dotted around Spain have been preserved – minus the slogan, however.

is, incidentally, one of the few that produces a table wine made from 100% Palamino grapes. It's made in a non-DO wine-making area and is called Castillo de San Diego, although everyone locally just calls it Barbadillo. It's a light easy-drinking wine.
Tours: Monday to Saturday, starting 12 noon and 1pm
Tel: 956 385 500
Address: C Luis de Eguilaz 11

Bodegas Hidalgo originally stood on the sea-shore when it was first built. This has been a family-run business since 1792, and they make exceptional wines, the best-known of which is La Gitana, named after the gypsy lover of the winery's founder. They also produce an excellent *manzanilla pasada* called Pastrana. And their VORS wine list is long, too. To check out their full range, head for their shop and visitor centre.
Tel: 956 385 304
Address: C Banda Playa 24

Bodegas de Velasco is a small jolly place near the market (itself well worth a visit) that

serves their manzanilla called La Cigarrera straight from the butt.
Open: Monday to Friday, 8am to 3pm
Address: C Truco s/n

La Abuela Lola is a *despacho de vinos*, stocking all the local wines and also running tastings.
Address: C Caballeros 21

DO Montilla-Moriles

The bodegas in this DO make their wines using the same solera method as in Jerez, and they also refer to their wines as finos, amontillados and olorosos. This has been a source of angst and friction between the two *consejos*: these terms cannot be used by Montilla-Moriles in the UK, for example, and by and large Montilla-Moriles has had a struggle on its hands to distinguish itself from its better-known rival.

The first thing to note about wines from Montilla-Moriles is that the Pedro Ximénez grape is used for all the *generosos* – not the

Julian Sanjuan

Palomino that is used down the road in Jerez. Second, the deliciously dry, light, herby-tasting finos are not fortified with alcohol: they reach 15.5% naturally, thanks to the oven-like temperatures here throughout the summer. And everyone here will tell you that the lack of fortification means you don't get a hangover.

Montilla-Moriles also produces young white table wine called *jóven afrutado*, using other grape varieties in addition to PX: Torrentes and Baladi to name just two. And they are now experimenting with red wine, too: look out for Marenas, a wine made by José Márquez Herrador who hails from Montilla.

The wines from this DO all tend to be drunk locally, rather than shipped abroad, so, if time allows, do try and discover some of them for yourself – they're extremely quaffable.

Montilla

Alvear is the oldest and biggest wine business in the Montilla-Moriles DO. It was founded in 1729 and is still family-owned. The bodega is in the middle of Montilla (a pleasant little town with a wine museum) and is affectionately called La Monumental by the locals. It's an attractive complex, with palm-lined courtyards and bougainvillea scrambling up whitewashed walls, and includes a vineyard for experimental vines – which used to be the town's football field.
Tel: 957 650 100
Address: Av María Auxiliadora 1, Montilla

Gracia Hermanos bodega is situated in an old flour mill next to Montilla's railway station. Try their María del Valle fino and Oloroso cream – both are delicious.
Tel: 957 650 162
Address: Av Márques de la Vega de Armijo 4, Montilla

Aguilar de la Frontera

Toro Albala, some 50 kilometres from Córdoba, is a small but distinguished bodega that used to be an old power station: one of their finos is called Eléctrico. Other wines to try are their award-winning Fino del Lagar and sweet Don PX. The bodega also has a wonderful museum featuring over 2000 books on wine.
Tel: 957 660 046
Address: Ctra Córdoba-Málaga s/n, Aguilar de la Frontera
Website: www.talbala.com

You may also like to consult the exhaustive website at www.montilla-moriles.org. It is all in Spanish, but the addresses are pretty easy to figure out.

DO Málaga

The wines from Málaga tell the familiar tale of a golden age when Mountain Wine, as it was known in Victorian times, added a glow to faces in drawing rooms around the world. But then disaster struck. The industry was first brought to its knees by phylloxera (a nasty vine-munching weevil); and later it was dealt a blow by the arrival of mass tourism, which saw vineyards on the coast ripped up to make way for high-rise hotels – bricks and mortar, after all, have a far higher yield than a few vines.

And so these delicious top-quality wines, with the flavours, colours and finger-sucking stickiness of deconstructed Christmas cake, simply ceased to be available.

But you can't keep wine-makers from their passion, and Málaga still produces some superb wines, ranging from pale-yellow dry PXs, to intensely sweet almost-black Moscatels.

The DO covers three main areas: an area on the coast and inland to the west of the city, around Estepona; the coast east of the city as far as the province of Granada; and inland around the Axarquía region. The grapes used are always Pedro Ximénez and Moscatel, which are frequently sun-dried to increase their sugar content before they are pressed. These wines are fortified and aged using the solera-criadera system, so you won't find the vintage year on the bottle.

They are, however, categorised according to age: wines are labelled Málaga if aged between 6 months and 2 years; Noble, if between 2 years and 3 years; Añejo, between 3 years and 5 years; and Transañejo if aged over 5 years.

Palido, incidentally, is a moscatel wine that is put through the solera system but not aged.

Málaga bodegas

Okay, you've got the knowledge and now you'd like to try some wines. Alas, things have suffered on the retail front, too. The number of bodegas left is a fraction of what there was in the region's heyday. And, in contrast to Jerez and its sister towns in the sherry triangle, there are very few that you can visit.

In part, this is a consequence of Málaga DO regulations, which at one time said that wines had to be aged in the city. Since Málaga is such a tourist hot-spot, with land values high, many of the old bodegas were sold off, and the barrels moved to faceless industrial zones on the outskirts – places only a really dedicated wine-hound would want to visit.

Still, help is at hand, with two branches of **Museo del Vino Málaga** – a combined wine merchant's and educational centre – in Mijas and Ojén. You can wander in for a wine-tasting with tapas at any time (for a small charge), and then admire not just the wines but also a range of local pottery and wine paraphernalia that's all for sale. The buildings themselves are also of some interest: the branch in Mijas, for example, used to be the local electricity station. But best of all, the staff are incredibly enthusiastic and knowledgeable about wine and the area. The shops are open seven days a week throughout the year, 11am to 3pm, and 4.30pm to 8pm (but the afternoon times move back an hour in the summer). Groups requiring a wine-tasting should book in advance.
Mijas branch: C San Sebastián s/n; tel: 952 486 367
Ojén branch: C Carrera 39; tel: 952 881 453
Web: www.museovinomálaga.net

Here are a few other names you should keep an eye out for, from the DO Málaga:

Garijo is a traditional bodega established in the nineteenth century. They only use oak barrels, not steel tanks, and everything is done in the old-fashioned way. Their Pedro Ximénez recently won a first prize in Italy.

Gomara is one of the largest bodegas in the area, and you'll commonly find their wines in the supermarkets.

Jarel is a boutique producer whose wine was served at Prince Felipe of Spain's wedding. In other words, their moscatels are good – very good, in fact.

López Hermanos produce a premium range that includes a PX solera from 1920, and a light PX that is aged for 18 months in new French oak – an exception as everyone else ages their PX in old oak.

Quitapenas, founded in 1880, is a very well-known bodega in Málaga: the founder was a great philanthropist. They have three taverns in the city: the main one is on C Marín García – look out for the barrels outside the front door.

DO Sierras de Málaga

As the name suggests, this DO covers the mountainous region behind Málaga, where a new generation is currently rediscovering what everyone since the Romans had always known full well: that Málaga province is ideal vine-growing country.

Here they make dry unfortified wines – red, white and rosé – using grapes we are all more familiar with, such as Tempranillo and

Cabernet Sauvignon, Chardonnay and Riesling – plus a few local varieties just to keep things interesting. Ronda in particular is a bit of a wine hot-spot at the moment: there's a wine equivalent of a gold rush going on, although fortunes tend to be spent rather than made on wine.

Some key names from DO Sierras de Málaga:

Cooperativa Virgen de la Oliva, not surprisingly, sell olive oil as well as wine – the latter goes under the name of Tierras de Mollina. Their red wine is 100% Shiraz and is called Gadea; the white is a Moscatel called Montespejo. Their posh wine is a PX and Moscatel blend called Carpe Diem.

Príncipe Alfonso de Hohenlohe is one of two producers making a Petit Verdot wine. This grape used to be found in a Bordeaux blend, but many of these tricky-to-grow vines have been torn out in France now. The bodega at Cortijo de las Monjas is open to the public and runs wine tasting tours – telephone 952 114 124 for further details.

Vetas Martín, who used to be the wine-maker for Príncipe Alfonso, produced 600 bottles of red wine last year, retailing at serious prices, including a 100% Petit Verdot.

Descalzos Viejos produce a very good, just about affordable, blend. The bodega, in a restored eleventh-century convent, is a joint venture between a Ronda architect and an Argentinian wine-maker.

Bodega Los Bujeos makes a wine called Pasoslargos. The owner also runs the very trendy restaurant in Ronda called El Tragabuches.

Finally, **Bodega F Schatz** has been pioneering not just wines in the area, but organic wines, for the last twenty years. What's the big deal about organic wines? Well, there is something very end-of-the-rainbow about this bodega. It's a colour-saturated sun-filled spot full of happy vines, happy animals, and with a wine-maker wrapped up in completing the circle, not just with his wines but also with the ecology of the place. Chickens and songbirds keep the insect populations under control, cats keep the mice at bay. Nets keep birds off the fruit as it ripens (undamaged grapes are essential to good wine) but then the second flush of grapes are left on the vines for them to feed on. The soil is everything, and it is kept nitrogenated with clover and other fixing plants grown between the vine rows. And the yeasts used in the fermentation process come naturally from the environment. The result is a classy – and not cheap – range of seven wines using some very untypical grapes for Spain, including Riesling, Trollinger, Spaetburgunder, Lemberger, Petit Verdot and Muskattrollinger, as well as the more usual Tempranillo, Syrah, Merlot, Cabernet Sauvignon and Chardonnay. Because the sugars in these wines are completely fermented, they are all dry – but each style tastes unique, not only because of the grapes, but also the soil in which they grow. And there is something about the organic method that makes the flavours and aromas really dance out of the wine glass. The Tinto reminds you of plain chocolate, vanilla and cinnamon; the Petit Verdot by contrast has the smack of hot dry herbs. As for whites, the Riesling 2001 has to be one of the best examples in Spain, and the Chardonnay is marvellously crisp with subtle oaking. The bodega isn't normally open to the public, but if you are prepared to buy a minimum of a

Córdoba

case, then ring to arrange a visit.
Tel: 952 871 313
Address: Finca La Sanguijuela Aptdo.
Correos 131, Ronda
Web: www.f-schatz.com

DO Condado de Huelva

Condado de Huelva wines have a historical claim to fame: they were the first wines to be drunk in the New World, since Christopher Columbus set sail from Huelva with local wine in his hold. Huelva also used to supply grapes to Jerez, before the regulatory council there decided that all grapes had to be supplied from within the Jerez DO.

But tastes have changed, and strawberries are now a more profitable crop than grapes, so the wine industry has suffered. The DO covers quite a large area of Huelva province,

but it isn't as extensive as it once was. From the mid 1980s to the present day, the vineyard area has been reduced from 20,000 hectares to just 6,000. Still, Huelva does continue to make *generosos* as well as table wines.

Even though they are eclipsed by their counterparts in Jerez, there are some very good fortified wines in this area. Recently, however, there has been a change of emphasis towards young white wines made with the Zalema grape: this is popular with wine-growers because it's a high yielding variety, and, although it doesn't result in an especially interesting wine used on its own, it does generally produce better young whites than those made with the Palomino grape in Jerez.

Zalema accounts for about 80% of Huelva's production. The other grape varieties that are allowed to be used are: Palomino Fino,

Listán de Huelva, Garrido Fino, Moscatel de Alejandria and Pedro Ximénez.

A few years ago, the regional government set up an experimental vineyard to see how different wine varieties adapted to the local conditions. The idea was to promote other wines, both white and red, and hopefully inject a bit of extra life into what is one of the least dynamic DOs in Spain. The white Colombard grape is gaining some acceptance, because it maintains its acidity in spite of the hot summer weather; as for red grapes, Tempranillo has been planted by some growers, along with smaller quantities of Shiraz and Merlot.

There are five categories of wine in Huelva:

Condado de Huelva, cheerful plonk that you buy in bulk.

Condado de Huelva Jóven, table wines made from the Zalema grape. The alcohol content is between 10.5 and 12.5%.

Condado Palido, fino-style wine produced using the solera method – the better ones being made from Palomino Fino and Garrido Fino grapes. The alcohol content is higher than the table wines, varying between 15 and 17%. The wines are aged for a minimum of three years.

Condado Viejo, similar to oloroso in undergoing oxidative ageing, and usually made from Zalema grapes, although Listán de Huelva, Palomino Fino and Garrido Fino varieties are also used.

Generosos de Licor, which can be dry or sweet, and must be aged for at least two years. They are sold as pale dry, medium, cream and pale cream.

Condado bodegas

Vinicola del Condado is the largest
winery in the area. It's the biggest wine co-
operative in Andalucía, with around 1000
members, and produces nearly 20 million
litres of wine a year. Their best-known white
is Privilegio del Condado. Drunk chilled, it's
light and slightly fruity, and it slips down very
nicely having only around 10% alcohol.
Drunk on a rainy day in northern Europe,
though, it might seem a bit on the bland side.
They also have a new red Lantero. This is a
young, very pleasant wine made with 100%
Tempranillo, with aromas of raspberry and
blackberry.
Tel: 959 410 261
Address: C San José 2, Huelva
Web: www.vinicoladelcondado.com

Bodegas Andrade

This smaller concern also produces an
agreeable white, Castillo de Andrade. But
probably more interesting are their fortified
wines, especially a Condado Viejo called
Doceañero.
Tel: 959 410 106
Address: Av Coronación 35, Huelva

You may also like to check out further
information on the history of the DO at
their website:
www.vinoscondadohuelva.com

Non-DO: the Vinos de la Tierra of Granada province

Within Granada province, there are three
main growing areas, each with a *Vinos de la
Tierra* classification. Production is on a small
scale and the wines vary in quality, but as each
of the main wine-growing areas of Granada
has its own particular charm, a visit in search of
a few *bodegas* is well worth a day out. The
spectacular scenery of the southern slopes of
the Sierra Nevada is home to the wines of the
Contraviesa-Alpujarra, which consists of
less than a dozen bodegas spread through
several small towns and villages. Some of these
wines are produced from Europe's highest
growing grapes – the vines are protected from
north winds by the Sierra Nevada. Much of
the wine produced is simple *vino costa*, a rosé-
type wine that should be drunk immediately.

The wines of **Norte de Granada** come
from Granada's cave country around the
town of Guadix. Many of the wines here are
just for home consumption, and the
unlabelled bottle that lands on your table at
lunchtime is likely to be the proprietor's own
wine. Don't have wildly high expectations,
and you'll be agreeably surprised how well it
goes with the home-style cooking.

The red and white wines of **Granada
Suroeste** come from between Almuñecar

and Motril on the coast, and from inland as far as the Lecrín valley, halfway towards the city of Granada. There are several bodegas to visit in this area, but here are two examples whose wines are really interesting, even though they do not qualify for DO status.

Motril
Bodegas Horacio Calvente
Horacio Calvente is not a man who shirks a challenge: he admits that he has "always liked difficult things." A fruit grower from Jete, just behind the resort of Almuñecar on Granada's Costa Tropical, he became interested in wine-making and several years ago started buying up small plots of well-established vines that had fallen into disuse in the striking and mountainous Sierra de Cázulas nearby.

The scenery may be beautiful but the going is tough: the grapes are grown up to 1000 metres above sea level on terraced slopes where it's impossible to use vehicles or machinery – the work is done with the aid of two mules. And the challenge he has set himself and his small team doesn't end there. Most of the vines are about an hour's drive from the bodega, and some plots are also an hour's walk from others. However, there is method in this apparent madness. Horacio has chosen his small plots of vineyard carefully, with careful thought as to the microclimate and its effect upon the grapes and their ripening: "There is a 15 degrees centigrade difference between the coast and here," he says. "The high altitude means more moderate temperatures and there is also the cooling effect of the sea."

Despite these difficult conditions, his small but well-equipped and modern bodega now produces 40,000 to 50,000 bottles of wine a year. There are two reds: Márques de Cázulas, made from Tempranillo, Garnacha

and Cabernet Sauvignon grapes and aged for six months in oak to produce a very fruity and full-bodied wine; and Calvente, made from Tempranillo, Shiraz, Cabernet Sauvignon and Merlot grapes to produce a full, deep and spicy wine. These are now receiving serious attention from wine experts in Spain, and are available in some bars and restaurants in the city of Granada and around the province.

And the future? Well, despite the bodega having a small output, Horacio's intention is to "carry on making the best wine possible – not a greater variety of wines, nor a greater increase in production." And he is up for another challenge: the possibility of cultivating a variety of grape that he says has never been grown in Spain before. But he won't give any clues as to what it is – you'll just have to wait and see.

Ctra Almería 16, Motril
Tel: 958 603 013
Website:www.bodegasmar.com

Villamena
Bodegas Señorio de Nevada

"My wine-making is not just a business," says José Pérez Arco, proprietor of Bodegas Señorio de Nevada, "but a passion: a dream to create the best possible wine from here."

Some fifteen or so kilometres from the city of Granada, in the heart of the Lecrín valley, dubbed the Valley of Happiness by the Moors of Granada and once the burial ground of their kings, Señor Pérez Arco's vines can leaf and fruit against a stunning backdrop of mountains and the snowy slopes of the Sierra Nevada.

His wine-making came about by accident when, with a view to retiring from business in Germany, he bought a property that came planted with vines. As a lover of fine wines he hadn't the heart to pull them up, and he decided to see what he could make with a

harvest. The first wines were a considerable investment. Now, nearly ten years on, the wines are made in a state-of-the-art bodega. Four grape varieties are used to produce two reds, which spend ten to twelve months in oak: a principally Cabernet and Merlot blend, with Tintilla de Granada (a local Tempranillo) added; and a Syrah and Merlot blend which also has some Tintilla de Granada.

The 100,000 bottle output is produced without the need for pesticides and herbicides because of the dry spring and summer months. The microclimate and the mineral-rich soil of the valley have a big influence on the quality of the wines produced. "The summers are warm to hot here," José Pérez Arco explains, "but at night the temperature drops to 12 degrees, which is great for a slow ripening of the grapes. The Sierra Nevada protects the vines from northerly winds, and the nearby Mediterranean has a moderating effect on both the summer heat and the winter cold."

Once the grapes are harvested, the care given to the wines-to-be is exceptional: the French and American oak barrels in which the wines are maturing are topped up weekly to keep out air, and for the ten to twelve month period that the wines are in oak the barrels are emptied and cleaned every three months before being refilled.

And the hard work pays off. José Pérez Arco's full-bodied, smooth and fruity wines have won national and international prizes, are sold in the prestigious El Corte Inglés department store, and are on the wine lists of paradors. His dream seems to have come true.

Ctra de Conchar s/n, Cortijo del Camino Real, 18659 Villamena, Valle del Lecrín
Tel: 958 777 092

Spirits

Three spirits dominate in Andalucía: anise, brandy and rum. That's obviously not to say you won't find people drinking others – of course you will. But these are very definitely the local favourites.

Anise, *aguardiente*

Pliny the Elder wrote that anise cured indigestion, brought about restful sleep and helped to get rid of wrinkles. It is doubtful whether Pliny's school of thought was directly responsible, but anise-flavoured spirits are certainly popular all around the Mediterranean.

Anise is in fact something of a national beverage in Spain. It's imbibed by elderly gentlemen with their morning coffee, and it's especially popular around Christmas time served alongside a plate of sweetmeats. It is usually distilled from the grape mash that's left over from wine-making, but it can also be made from rectified cane spirits. This latter

method was necessary when phylloxera, the bug that devours vine roots, wiped out the local vineyards in the nineteenth century, and producers were forced to find alternative supplies. These days, distillers produce a bewildering array of fruit-, nut- and chocolate-flavoured anise spirits that are less alcoholic than the original fire-water.

Anise-producing areas in Andalucía include: Rute and Montilla in Córdoba province, and Huelva province, where the anise from the iron-mining areas is called *aguardiente de hierro*, or iron anise. It was thought at one time that anise helped clear miners' lungs. Needless to say, this aguardiente is very dry and very alcoholic. However, the town of Cazalla in Seville province is probably the most famous anise-producer. Indeed, anise is often called *Cazalla* (ask for it in Peru, and they'll know what you mean), and the town has been making and exporting the stuff for centuries.

Examine a shelf of anise bottles and you'll notice that the labels are decorated with very folksy imagery (gnomes, flowers and so on). Carmen Ladrón, who has been restoring her Carthusian monastery for the last 20 years or so, and is now something of an expert on the monks' lifestyle, has an interesting explanation for these designs. Cazalla became a centre of anise production thanks to Carthusian monks, whose liqueur-making skills have always been legendary (think Green Chartreuse). But when the monasteries were confiscated and the distilleries sold off, the traditional monastic imagery on the bottle labels was an uncomfortable reminder of the monks now begging in the streets. So the labels were radically redesigned, in this secular folksy style, in an effort to blank the whole unsavoury episode from people's memories.

Brandy, *coñac*

The word brandy comes from the Dutch *brandewijn* – burnt wine – which is what the Dutch traders called the spirit when they first introduced it into northern Europe from southern France and Spain in the sixteenth century. The origins of the drink can be traced back to the Arab alchemists who were experimenting with distilling grapes and other fruits in order to make medicinal spirits. Grape brandy is distilled from fermented grape juice, or crushed (but not pressed) grape pulp and skin. It is aged in wooden casks, usually oak, and it is this that gives brandy its colour and helps to develop more complex flavours and aromas. More grape brandy is produced in Spain than in any other European country; and of that production, some 95% comes from Andalucía, especially from Málaga.

Brandy de Jerez is made in the sherry triangle, using the same solera method as sherries – and this is what differentiates it from all other brandies, including Cognac. The solera system involves the continuous blending of young brandies with older ones through a series of oak barrels previously used for maturing sherry. Virtually all Brandy de Jerez, however, is made from wines produced elsewhere in Spain – primarily from the Airen grape in La Mancha and Extremadura – as the local sherry grapes are all needed for sherry production. Nowadays most of the distilling is also done elsewhere in Spain; but the brandy is then shipped to Jerez for ageing in the soleras. Naturally enough, Brandy de Jerez has its own Consejo Regulador, and there are three possible categories for the brandy:

Solera which has been aged for at least six months

Solera Reserva which has been aged for at least a year

Solera Gran Reserva which has been aged for at least three years.

Seville

Because the sherry bodegas use their own distillates, and barrels that have had different kinds of sherry in them, these brandies are all unique – and gorgeous tasting. This is the kind of after-dinner tipple you can happily drink and drink, and not realise how much you've had till you try to stand up. It's a soft, smooth, beautifully rounded spirit.

For the Solera Gran Reserva brandies, many of which will actually have aged for ten years or more, the bodegas tend to go to town on the packaging. Here are some favourite examples, for both taste and exotic plumage:

Cardenal Mendoza (Sánchez Romate) was originally produced in 1887 for the exclusive use of the Sánchez Romate family and their friends, and it's still made according to the same family recipe. The simple clear bottle has an ornate, colourful label, and is packed in a genuine cork box.

Conde de Osborne (Osborne) has the remarkable prestige of having both its bottle and its label created by Salvador Dalí in 1964.

Gran Duque de Alba (Williams & Humbert) comes in a curvy opaque bottle; at the centre of the label, circled in gold, is a portrait of the eponymous Grand Duke.

Lepanto (González Byass) was named after the sixteenth-century battle in which Spain defeated the Ottoman fleet, and is bottled in a hand-painted crystal decanter topped off with a gold-patterned stopper.

My own absolute favourite, however, is rather more discreetly packaged: Fernando de Castilla's **Único Solera Gran Reserva**.

About the only way most people can afford these brandies is to order a glass in a restaurant. A great fuss will generally be made of you if you do, and of the brandy, too: the glass is likely to be gently warmed over a candle. You could be entitled to feel that these spirits are too good to be subjected to this kind of treatment; you may even be tempted to play the spoilsport and not allow the waiters to do their stuff.

But half the fun of brandy, I think, is in the ritual of it: the swirling and the sniffing, and the cupping of the glass in both hands. To get the most out of this little ceremony, pour yourself a smallish measure into a balloon-shaped glass (tumblers and wine glasses just won't do). You've judged the right amount if the brandy doesn't spill out when you tilt the glass horizontally.

Rum, *ron*

No, rum wasn't invented in the Caribbean: it is Andalucía (and in particular the region from Málaga to Motril) that takes the credit, and it was probably the first spirit drink ever produced here. It is made from sugar cane: a tall, coarse-grained grass that was a primary source of sugar for the sweet-toothed Arabs. The by-product of boiling and centrifuging off sugar crystals is a sticky black stuff called molasses. Yeast particles tend to get stuck in this gummy gloop and – hey presto! – fermentation happens. This rapidly produces a sort of sweet wine which is then distilled into rum.

Sugar cane, however, much prefers to grow in the conditions in the Caribbean where Columbus took it from the Canary Islands on his second voyage – although the Caribbean rum industry didn't really get going until the seventeenth century. All the same, small quantities of rum are still produced in the Motril area: try and track down the Francisco Montero Martín brand.

What to cook and how to cook it

Cooking andaluz

Andalucian recipes

A while ago, I dropped into a Spanish friend's home around lunchtime and, of course, I was invited to share their meal – which happened to be a lentil, chorizo and morcilla stew. Her little boy was tucking happily into his blood sausage, and it struck me then how amazingly robust and healthy the cooking in this part of the world is.

Andalucian cooks use the freshest and best ingredients at their disposal, whether it's olive oil, or the choicest chorizo, or that day's fish catch from the market. So they tend to be relaxed about their recipes (or inventive – depending on your point of view), since they always start with what's available and fresh. In this section you'll

sometimes find not just a recipe, but suggested variations around that theme.

I'm a recent convert to sherry and think it's an ideal partner for food. A brief and thoroughly unscientific survey amongst family and friends revealed that everyone is fairly confident about wine these days, but sherry is still a bit of a mystery for most tipplers – so at the end of the recipes I've added a suggestion for suitable accompaniments, where appropriate.

Lastly, a note on utensils: heavy, deep-sided frying-pans are essential in the Spanish kitchen, and they can also double as paella pans. *Cazuelas* are earthenware casserole dishes that are unglazed on the outside.

They're ideal for all the one-pot cooking that goes on, but they're not suited to electric or induction hobs. And remember to soak them in water before using them for the first time, otherwise they'll crack.

Pestle and mortars are commonly used, and they're great if you've got the time. Food processors make a speedier alternative, of course, but the texture of the sauce or soup won't be as good. If you're into pulses, it makes sense to buy them dried, not tinned, but this does mean one heck of a lot of boiling. Andalucian cooks are therefore rather fond of pressure cookers, to reduce cooking times. I have to say I've never really mastered the physics of these, preferring a long slow simmer, to beans all over the ceiling – and it's my low-tech approach that is usually reflected in the recipes.

The selection that follows merely scratches the surface of all the wonderful dishes to be discovered, and I hope they'll inspire you to start adding Andalucian food to your culinary repertoire. Enjoy.

These recipes are for four people, unless otherwise stated.

Key to sherry symbols

(FM) Fino or manzanilla

(A) Amontillado

(O) Dry oloroso

(PC) Palo cortado

(C) Cream and sweet oloroso

(PX) Pedro Ximénez

Soup dishes

Garlic soup

sopa de ajo

I had this for supper one chilly November evening in Jaén – it's deliciously warming, thanks to the garlic and cayenne. Most recipes stipulate water, but if you've got some chicken stock to hand, so much the better. Jamón leftovers are another option, particularly if you're using water, to give a bit more oomph to the flavour.

50ml olive oil
4 large cloves of garlic, minced
100g breadcrumbs
2 tsp paprika
1/4 tsp cayenne pepper, or to taste
1 tsp salt, or a few nuggets of serrano ham
1 litre of water
2 large eggs, beaten
1 tbsp chopped parsley

Heat the olive oil over a gentle heat in a heavy saucepan or casserole dish. Add the garlic and let it soften for a few minutes, without letting it brown, and then stir in the breadcrumbs. Increase the heat slightly, and fry everything until it's golden, stirring frequently to prevent the crumbs from burning rather than toasting. Add the paprika, cayenne and salt (or ham), followed by the water. Bring to the boil and simmer for 20 minutes.

Take the soup off the heat and test the seasoning – you're looking for a spicy, sinus-clearing warmth – then stir though the egg mixture. Scatter parsley over the soup and serve immediately.

Málaga garlic soup

maimones

This soup is similar to the one above. The recipe was given to Heloise by the members of a flamenco troupe in a bar in the back streets of Málaga. Apparently the name of the soup comes from an Andalucian emir called Maimon.

50ml olive oil
4 cloves of garlic, chopped
4 slices of bread
1 litre of hot chicken stock

Sauté the garlic in the oil until it starts to turn slightly gold in colour. Add the slices of bread and fry on both sides until golden brown. Take four bowls, place a slice of bread and some garlic in each, and pour the chicken stock over. Finely chopped jamón serrano may also be added.

(FM)

Gazpacho

gazpacho

There are almost as many different versions of this recipe as there are cooks in Andalucía. But the key to making a good gazpacho is to experiment with the proportions of the ingredients until you have a soup to your taste: some people add fewer tomatoes, less garlic or bread, some add more water. For a better consistency use a pestle and mortar; but a blender does make the job a lot quicker and easier.

1 kg ripe tomatoes – the juicier the better
cucumber, about 20 cm in length
1 red pepper (or half a red and half a green pepper)
1 clove of garlic
1 large mild onion
1 small slice of country-style bread
1 tbsp wine vinegar
1 tbsp olive oil
pinch of salt

Pour boiling water onto the tomatoes and leave for five minutes, then skin and cut out their tough cores. Roughly chop and place in a blender along with the garlic, bread, oil, vinegar and salt. Peel and finely chop the cucumber, garlic and onion and set aside about one third of these to serve as a garnish for the gazpacho (this is not a very generous amount of cucumber, pepper and onion garnish – you may want to chop extra) and add the remainder to the ingredients in the blender. Blend until smooth. At this stage you may wish to add a little cold water to the gazpacho if you prefer it a little more dilute. Chill well before serving.

The cucumber, pepper and onion garnish usually comes to the table in separate little bowls, so people can add a little of what they want to their own dish of gazpacho. Croutons make a good additional garnish, and some cooks also add ice cubes for an extra refreshing soup at the height of summer.

Thick gazpacho

porra

This soup has the consistency of a dip. It's usually eaten (or slurped) cold as a starter but I've found other uses for it too: try spooning it over grilled chicken, or using it as a filling for a multi-layered aubergine cake.

100g red pepper
500g juicy tomatoes
150g stale country bread or baguette
100ml olive oil
50ml water
1 or 2 cloves of garlic
pinch of salt
4 eggs
a few small thin pieces of jamón serrano

Cut up the pepper, tomatoes and bread. Add the olive oil, water, garlic and salt, and blend until smooth and creamy. The consistency should be like that of taramasalata – you may need to add a little more water. Chill well. Before serving, hard-boil the eggs and, when cool, cut them into quarters. Having ladled the porra into bowls, dole out the egg quarters and the ham into each.

Green gazpacho

gazpacho verde

Green gazpachos hail from Huelva province and typically contain the herb coriander, betraying a Portuguese influence. There is no definitive recipe, and you'll come across variations with lettuce, basil, mint, parsley and even cucumber added to them. My version uses chicken stock (made from a decent cube) and I like it warm, because the weather was vile on the day I first tested the recipe and cold soup seemed like a penance. But it is equally good served chilled.

150g white bread, crusts removed
100g mix of coriander and basil leaves
2 plump cloves of garlic, crushed in a pinch of salt
75ml olive oil
1 tbsp sherry vinegar
1 litre of very hot chicken stock

Put the bread, herbs and garlic into a food processor and blitz until you have a herb and crumb mix. Keep the machine on and slowly add the oil and vinegar, followed by the chicken stock. Adjust the vinegar and salt seasoning and serve immediately.

White gazpacho

ajo blanco

This is a delicious soup. Please don't feel tempted to use ready-ground almonds: using whole ones will result in a much better flavour. The soup is usually garnished with peeled and seeded Moscatel grapes – but small, diced pieces of melon make a good alternative.

150g stale white country-style bread, crusts removed
150g whole almonds, peeled
3 cloves of garlic, sliced
½ tsp salt
150ml olive oil
1 litre of water
2 tbsp sherry vinegar (or more to taste)

Soak the bread in some water for a moment, squeeze out the excess, and then pop it into a food processor with the almonds, garlic and salt. Blitz until you've made a fairly smooth sauce. Leave the processor on while you slowly add the oil through the lid, followed by the water. You want the consistency of double cream, not porridge, so you may need to adjust the amount of water. Pour into a suitable bowl, season with the vinegar, and add more salt if necessary. Chill well before serving.

'Seville-style' fish soup

sopa sevillana

You'll come across this in lots of restaurants around Granada, not Seville. It's a light delicate soup, the success of which depends on a decent fish stock. See page 124 for details on how to make this.

1 litre of fish stock
100ml milk
100g peeled raw prawns
100g small pieces of white fish
100g peas
salt to taste

Bring the stock and milk to a very gentle simmer. Add the prawns, fish and peas. The soup is ready when these ingredients are cooked.

Chicken and vegetable broth

sopa de picadillo

This is one of my favourites – and it's one of
the most delicious soups to come out of
Andalucía's kitchens. The soup is traditionally
served with a couple of small mint leaves on
top.

2 carrots
2 leeks
2 sticks of celery
2 potatoes
1 onion
1 small chicken, jointed
1 fresh bayleaf
2 litres of water

to serve:
2 hard-boiled eggs, chopped
100g finely-chopped jamón serrano
some mint leaves

Quarter the vegetables and add to a large
saucepan along with the chicken and the
water. Simmer for about 45 minutes until
everything is cooked. Fish out the chicken
and strip the meat off the bones, returning
the pieces to the broth. Add the boiled egg
and ham and serve the soup with torn mint
leaves scattered over.

variation
Chickpeas are sometimes added.

Wild asparagus soup

sopa de esparragos trigueros
This soup is particularly popular in the Pueblos Blancos region of Cádiz. Naturally, cultivated asparagus makes an acceptable substitute, although it doesn't have quite the same intensity of flavour.

1 bunch of wild asparagus, about 300g
2 small slices of bread
4 cloves of garlic
50ml olive oil
salt
1½ litres of water or stock
4 eggs

Discard the tough ends of the asparagus stems and cut the rest into 2-3cm pieces. Heat the olive oil in a heavy-bottomed saucepan over a low heat and add the chopped garlic and bread. When the bread is golden, remove both the garlic and the bread, and mash them up with some salt in a mortar. Add the asparagus to the frying-pan and sauté for a few minutes. Then add the bread mixture, stirring well before covering with the water or stock. Bring to the boil and cook for 10-15 minutes. Gently break the eggs into a saucer and slip them into the soup – you don't want them to break – and when they are poached, serve immediately.

Salad dishes

Restaurant salads can often be something of a disappointment: the universal Andalucian *ensalada mixta* of tomato, chopped onion, green olives and tuna, piled onto overburdened plates of shredded iceberg lettuce, tinned sweetcorn, grated carrot and pickled beetroot – and even sometimes red cabbage – might satisfy in terms of quantity, but frankly it's more of a compost heap than an elegant combination of ingredients. Don't despair, though; here are some very good tapas salads.

Orange salad

ensalada de naranja
This is a very pretty-looking salad, which goes rather well with barbecued fish.

4 oranges
3 large salad onions
small handful of fresh mint leaves
50ml olive oil
2 tsp white wine or cider vinegar
pinch of salt

Peel and slice the oranges across the middle and place the round slices on a large plate. Finely chop the onion and the mint, and sprinkle this mixture over the orange slices. Whisk the oil, salt and vinegar together and pour this dressing over everything.

Puerto de Santa María

Summer salad

pipirrana

You'll come across this Andalucian salad
everywhere: it is reminiscent of a gazpacho
that hasn't been blended, and, like gazpacho,
it's best served chilled. The key to the recipe
is to chop everything into ½ cm pieces: apart
from that, it's simplicity itself.

4 large tomatoes
1 green pepper, de-seeded
1 cucumber
1 small mild onion
3 tbsp olive oil
1 tbsp white wine vinegar
pinch of salt

Rinse and chop all the vegetables into tiny
dice, then stir in the oil and vinegar and
sprinkle the salt over everything. Mix well
and then pop it all into the fridge until you're
ready to serve it.

Salt-cod and orange salad

remojón

There are numerous versions of this Lenten
salad, and here are four of them. If you can't
get hold of salt-cod, then baked fresh cod or
smoked cod make good substitutes.

200g de-salted salt-cod pieces (see page xx)
2 oranges
2 large salad onions
handful of black olives
3 tbsp olive oil

Cut the cod into small pieces and place in a
dish. Peel the oranges and slice them across
the middle into fine rounds, and then cut
these round slices in half and place them
with the cod. Chop the onion finely and add
to the dish. Add the olives. Dress with olive
oil, and mix.

variation 1

Add three chopped tomatoes and two
crumbled hard-boiled eggs.

variation 2

Many years ago this used to be served as a
delicious tapa all year round in a traditional
fishermen's bar, now defunct, in Fuengirola,
Málaga.

150g cooked fresh cod
2 tomatoes
1 green pepper
half a small onion
1 orange, peeled
100g green olives, stoned
4 tbsp olive oil
1 tsp white wine vinegar
pinch of salt

Chop the ingredients into small pieces, add
the oil and vinegar and mix well. Chill before
serving.

variation 3

Remojón can morph into *ensalada
malagueña*, with the addition of two cooked
sliced potatoes to the preceding recipe.

Winter salad

ensalada de invierno
Before there were year-round crops of salad grown under plastic, salads in winter had to be made out of ingredients preserved from the summer. Fuensanta from the Bodeguilla de al Lado in Granada gave me this recipe.

375g jar of roasted red peppers
1 tin of plum tomatoes
1 medium onion
4 hard-boiled eggs
3 tbsp olive oil
1 tbsp sherry vinegar
pinch of salt

Drain off the juice from the peppers and tomatoes. Slice the peppers and quarter the tomatoes. Finely chop the onion and slice the hard-boiled eggs. Whisk the oil and vinegar, add it to the salad, and sprinkle with salt. Gently fold the dressing through the ingredients and serve.

Octopus salad

ensaladilla de pulpo
This is another simple salad. Paca from the Bar Peña in Alcudia de Guadix gave me the recipe; again, it is best chilled before serving – and eaten with lots of bread to mop up the delicious juices.

200g boiled octopus
2 medium-sized tomatoes
half a small onion
2 tbsp olive oil
½ tbsp sherry vinegar
pinch of salt

Chop all the ingredients into small pieces, and mix them with the oil, vinegar and salt.

Egg dishes

Omelette

tortilla

Tortillas are more akin to an egg cake, rather than a foamy, crisped-edged French omelette. Omit the onion from this recipe if you prefer, and bear in mind that tortilla is often better, at room temperature, the next day. Serves 5-6.

12 eggs, beaten
2kg potatoes, thinly sliced
1kg onions, sliced
100ml olive oil

Sauté the onion until soft but not brown, then add the potatoes and continue to cook everything gently without browning. Tip the contents of the pan into the beaten eggs and leave for a few minutes. Put more oil in the frying-pan, add the egg mixture, and let it cook through. Halfway through, turn the tortilla over. Do this by placing a plate over the frying-pan and then flipping them both over. Not quite as tricky as it sounds, though some people just put the frying-pan under a moderate grill to finish the tortilla off.

Scrambled eggs with wild mushrooms

revuelto de setas

This is a common way of using mushrooms from the dehesa in Huelva, for example, and even if your fungi are the cultivated versions of the wild ones, it's still delicious. Quantities are per person:

100g wild mushrooms
2 tbsp olive oil
½ clove of garlic
2 large eggs
salt and black pepper

Clean the mushrooms carefully, ridding them of grit and wildlife, and tear them into small pieces. Heat the oil in a frying-pan and add the garlic and mushrooms. Sauté gently until all the water that the mushrooms release has evaporated. While this is happening, beat the eggs with a tiny amount of water and few grains of salt and black pepper to taste. Stir the eggs into the mushrooms and keep stirring until the eggs are only just set. Serve at once. Some people garnish this with fried bread and chopped parsley but, to be honest, buttered toast is great.

variation

Substitute the mushrooms with 100g blanched wild asparagus.

Flamenco eggs

huevos a la Flamenca
This has been a supper favourite in my family for years. We sometimes stir the eggs into the mixture at the end rather than attempting to bake everything.

50ml olive oil
1 onion, chopped
1 clove of garlic, crushed
150g serrano ham or bacon, chopped
1 red pepper, de-seeded and sliced
4 large tomatoes, peeled and chopped
4 large eggs
50g chorizo sausage, sliced
100g cooked peas
100g cooked green beans
salt and pepper
1 tbsp chopped parsley

Preheat the oven to 200°C, gas mark 6. In a frying-pan heat the oil and add the onion, garlic and ham or bacon pieces. Sauté for a few minutes, then add the red pepper and tomatoes. Continue cooking on a medium heat until the tomatoes are reduced to a thick sauce, which will take about 15 minutes. Stir in the chorizo, peas, and beans and transfer the mixture to a gratin dish. Break each egg into a saucer and slip it onto the mixture. Sprinkle with salt and pepper and chopped parsley. Bake everything in the oven for between 7 and 10 minutes – until the whites are set, but the yolks still runny.

Bread, rice and pasta dishes

Fried bread

migas
Migas are another example of the Andalucian gift for transforming ordinary bread into something delicious. Choose a loaf that's chewy: and to make migas successfully, the bread really needs to be stale to start with, and then dampened. Drizzle a small amount of water over the cubed stale bread, wrap it in a tea towel, and leave for 30 minutes or so. You want it to be damp, but not soggy. Some people soak the bread in water and then squeeze out the excess, but this is a bit of a faff.

1 loaf of stale country-style bread, crust on, cubed and dampened
4 cloves of garlic
100ml olive oil
150g chorizo, diced small

Heat the oil over a medium heat, add the bread cubes and fry, stirring all the time. The bread will disintegrate into crumbs. As these turn gold, add the chorizo pieces. The pimentón in the chorizo will help turn the bread a deeper, more inviting colour.

Serve with fried egg, boquerones, or anything you fancy. Migas are quite rich, so about a couple of tablespoons per person will be ample.

Rice recipes

Chef Willy Moya, who owns the specialist rice restaurant La Cartuja in Seville as well as the Poncio reviewed on page 18, has kindly given us the following three recipes. It's worth pointing out that one of the tricks with rice is always to use volume measurements rather than weight, and that is what he has done here.

Rice with red prawns

arroz con carabineros
These large prawns are called policemen in Spanish (the Latin is Aristeus antennatus, in case you want to make sure you choose the right variety). In this instance, decent fish stock is essential, and it's not difficult to make – honest.

2 tbsp olive oil
4 red prawns, peeled and uncooked
1 small red chilli pepper
2 cloves of garlic, sliced
100ml oloroso sherry
100g tomato frito (or passata)
9 cups of fish stock
4 saffron threads
4 cups of short-grained rice
salt and pepper

Make the stock out of a kilo of fish bones, fish heads and peelings from the prawns (all previously uncooked), by simmering them in 2½ litres of water for 25 minutes, with an onion, bouquet garni, a slug of fino, a celery stick and a carrot. Skim any scum off the top, and strain through a fine sieve.

Take the heads off the prawns and fry them in a tablespoon of olive oil in a paella pan with the chilli pepper and garlic. Deglaze with the oloroso. Add the tomato frito and cook for a few minutes. Add the saffron and 9 cups of the fish stock, and cook for a further 5 minutes.

Add the rice, salt and pepper and, without stirring, cook for 16 minutes. A few minutes from the end add the headless red prawns. Leave for ten minutes and then sprinkle a few drops of oloroso over the rice just before serving.

Soupy rice with partridge

arroz caldoso de perdiz
This makes a substantial lunch that demands a long walk afterwards.

4 partridges (cleaned)
200ml olive oil
1 head of garlic
1 onion, sliced
2 green peppers, sliced (long variety, not bell pepper)
1 red pepper, de-seeded and sliced
1 celery stalk, sliced
2 large flavoursome tomatoes, chopped
1 leek, sliced
100ml sherry vinegar
100ml manzanilla
25g fresh ginger
2 twigs of fresh thyme leaves
1 twig each of fresh rosemary and oregano
1 tbsp chopped parsley
salt and black pepper
4 cups of short-grained rice
9 cups of water, approx

Heat a large casserole dish over a moderate heat and fry the partridges in the oil until golden and then put to one side. Next, fry the whole unpeeled cloves of garlic with all the vegetables until soft, and then add the partridges, vinegar and manzanilla. Cook for a few minutes before adding the herbs and the ginger knob. Add enough water to cover the ingredients and cook until the partridges are tender. Then remove the herbs and ginger, add the rice, and cook for 16 minutes, stirring occasionally, making sure there is always sufficient liquid – if not, add a bit more to keep the rice wet.

La Cartuja de Cazalla

125

Crusted cod and cauliflower rice

arroz en costra de bacalao y coliflor
This makes a really good and unusual supper dish.

fish stock
100ml olive oil
300g salt-cod, de-salted
1 cauliflower, in walnut-sized florets
2 cloves of garlic, sliced
5 piquillo peppers, sliced lengthways
saffron
100ml fino sherry
4 cups of short-grained rice
salt, black pepper
2 eggs, beaten

Make a stock with the skin and bones of the salt-cod; or follow the advice for fish stock in the previous recipe.

Sauté the garlic, cod, cauliflower, piquillo peppers and saffron in the olive oil. Add the fino sherry and reduce a little before adding the rice and sufficient stock to cover the ingredients to double depth. Add salt and pepper and then bake the mixture, covered, in the oven at 200°C, gas mark 6, for 14 minutes.

Pour the eggs over the rice mixture. Don't stir them in, but place the casserole under a moderate grill for a few minutes to cook the eggs, and then serve immediately.

Almerian pasta and rabbit stew

gurullos con conejo
Gurullos, a speciality of Almería, are rice-shaped little pasta. They very rarely make it onto the menu in restaurants, but one place that does make delicious gurullos is Terraza Carmona in Vera (see page 10), and this is one of their recipes.

for the gurullos:
200g pasta flour
5 tbsp olive oil
1/4 tsp salt
water

4 cloves of garlic
1 dried red pepper
100ml olive oil
1tbsp parsley, chopped
4 saffron threads
1/2 tsp salt
1kg rabbit, jointed
1 onion, diced
1 green pepper, de-seeded and diced
2 tomatoes, chopped
1 litre of water
2 medium potatoes, peeled and halved
200g dried haricot beans, soaked
salt and pepper

First, make the gurullos. Put the flour, oil and salt into a food mixer and, using a flat paddle, start mixing the ingredients. Add water a teaspoon at a time until soft balls of dough start to form. If the dough becomes wet, don't panic, just add a little more flour. Tip the dough out onto a floured surface and knead for a couple of minutes. It should feel soft and slightly springy. Wrap in clingfilm and chill for 30 minutes: this helps the gluten in the flour to relax, making the dough more elastic.

Cut the dough into two pieces to make it easier to roll out. Then either use your pasta-making machine to flatten each dough ball to the thickness of Italian tagliatelle pasta, or use a rolling pin, twisting the sheet of pasta through 90° frequently. Next use a pastry cutter or sharp knife to slice the dough into thin strips. Snip them into tiny pieces, each the size of a large grain of rice. Spread the gurullos flat on a tray to dry while you cook the rabbit and vegetable mixture.

Simmer the haricot beans in plenty of unsalted water until they are just cooked.

Fry the garlic and the dried red pepper in a little of the olive oil until the garlic has softened. If you don't have a dried red pepper, substitute it with a scant tablespoon of unsmoked sweet paprika. Scrape this mixture into a pestle and mortar and add the parsley, salt and saffron. Pound the ingredients into a paste.

In a deep-sided, heavy frying-pan or cazuela, brown the rabbit in the rest of the oil before adding the onion, green pepper and the tomatoes. Sauté for another five minutes or so until the veggies have collapsed a little. Add the water, haricot beans, potatoes, and garlic paste to the pan and season to taste.

Leave everything to simmer gently for 20 minutes, then 5 minutes before the end of the cooking time, add the gurullos. Let the stew cool a little before serving.

Vegetable dishes

Bean recipes

Andalucians are big bean eaters. There are several recipes here, and it won't take you long to realise that they are all largely variations on a theme. Basically, you chuck into a large pot whatever you've got in your larder or fridge, and then simmer everything until it's cooked. Do this often enough, and you'll end up with your own favourite combinations. But the recipes here should give you some inspiration, just to get you started.

Bean and chestnut stew

caldereta con judias y castañas
Pepe Gómez described this recipe to me on a drive up to Jabugo. The bean, chestnut and ham combination is typical of the Sierra de Aracena, and it's subsequently become a favourite winter supper in my family, served with grilled sausages. Do try and make this in Seville orange season – the juice gives the stew a wonderful subtle tang.

250g haricot beans, soaked overnight
1 bayleaf
50ml olive oil
1 onion, diced
1 clove of garlic, crushed
1 stick of celery
130g bacon, sliced (or 70g jamón serrano bits)
1 carrot, cut into chunks
200g jar of chestnuts
200g butternut squash, peeled and cut into 2cm cubes
1 large potato, peeled and cubed
100g chorizo sausage, cubed
1 cinnamon stick
$^1/_4$ tsp ground cloves
1 large twig of thyme
$1^1/_2$ litres of chicken stock, approx
juice of one Seville orange (or 1 tsp sherry vinegar)
small bunch of parsley, chopped

Boil the beans with the bayleaf in unsalted water until they are nearly cooked. How long this takes depends on how old the beans are! Discard the water and rinse the beans.

While the beans are simmering, heat the oil in a heavy-bottomed saucepan or casserole dish and make a sofrito with the onion, garlic and celery. Once the mixture has softened, fry the bacon for a few minutes before adding the beans, carrot, chestnuts, squash, potato, chorizo and the spices. Add enough stock to submerge everything and leave to simmer for around 35 minutes until the beans, potato and squash are tender. Just before serving, stir in the Seville orange juice and the parsley.

Beans with ham

habas con jamón

This is a classic tapa that hails from Granada, best when the broad beans are new and small (but you could use frozen at a pinch). Don't add salt if you use the jamón.

1 small onion
3 tbsp olive oil
450g shelled broad beans
100g jamón, finely diced, or bacon
100ml water or white wine

Soften the onion in oil until translucent. Add the ham and fry for 5 minutes before adding the beans and water or wine. Simmer gently until the beans are cooked and the liquid has reduced to a sauce.

Andalucian meat and vegetable pottage

cocido andaluz

There are infinite variations to this dish: basically, you throw what you've got in the larder into the pot. Pumpkin is a common addition in Andalucía, and you can also buy packs of pre-selected veg for your cocido, which will usually include leek, turnip, celery and carrot.

250g chickpeas, soaked overnight
300g stewing beef, or 1kg chicken pieces
1 ham bone
150g tocino (or pork belly)
100g ham
stock vegetables: one each of leek, small turnip, carrot and celery stick

2 cloves of garlic
1 tomato
4 peppercorns
4 saffron threads
1 small bunch of parsley
1 slice of bread

250g green beans, sliced
100g pumpkin or squash, diced
250g potatoes, diced

Put the chickpeas, meat, ham bone and stock vegetables into a large saucepan and cover with water. Bring to the boil, remove the froth, and simmer until the chickpeas and meat are tender.

Pour boiling water over the tomato and leave for five minutes. The skin can then be peeled off easily with a knife.

Pound the tomato, garlic, black pepper, saffron, bread and parsley with a pestle and mortar. Add a little bit of stock to slacken the mixture, and return it to the pot. Add the beans, pumpkin and potato, and cook for another 20 minutes or so. In summer and autumn, some cooks add slices of quince or pear at this stage.

Serve the soup first, followed by the meat and vegetables.

Thistle stew

berza de cardillo y tagarninas

This is popular in the Pueblos Blancos region of Andalucía. If you haven't got thistle leaves to hand (and let's face it, unless you're Eeyore it's unlikely), try thinly-sliced artichoke hearts. They have a similar flavour, although of course the stew will have a different texture if you make this substitution.

This dish is usually eaten as two separate courses. First you eat the pulses with the thistles, and then you serve the meat, black pudding and the pork fat. In Andalucía, people like to cut off a bit of each piece of meat, cut it up finely and mix it all together. The mixture is known as pringá and it is usually eaten on a thick slice of bread.

300g white beans
200g chickpeas
250g thistle leaves
250g stewing pork
100g tocino (or pork belly)
1 black pudding
2-3 cloves of garlic
1 dessertspoon paprika (mild)
100ml olive oil
1 tsp cumin
salt to taste

Soak the beans and chickpeas overnight in fresh water. In a large pan, add the beans, chickpeas, sliced thistles, pork, tocino and black pudding. Cover with water and cook with the lid firmly on.

Meanwhile, in a mortar, make a paste with the garlic, paprika, cumin and salt. Add to the pan, stirring in well. Cook on a low heat for 15 minutes with the lid off.

Pepe Gómez' bean stew

berza de alubias

Berza is the name given in Cádiz to this kind of one-pot veggie stew. It's a lunchtime dish, and Pepe, who is from El Puerta de Santa María, recommends a long walk along the beach afterwards. He also suggests using a pressure cooker for speed, and points out that you can substitute whatever veggies are in season for the swiss chard if you need to.

200g chickpeas soaked
200g haricot beans, soaked
20cm length of morcilla, cut in half
2 chorizos, halved
2 cloves of garlic
1/2 tsp salt
1 tsp peppercorns
1 tbsp paprika
2 large potatoes, diced
500g swiss chard, sliced
half a bunch of celery, sliced

Boil the chickpeas in about 2 litres of unsalted water for around 30 minutes, taking the scum off if necessary. Then add the haricot beans and simmer for another 30 minutes before adding the celery, morcilla and chorizo pieces. Use a pestle and mortar to crush the garlic, peppercorns, salt and paprika, and scrape this paste into the pot. When the beans are nearly tender, add the potatoes and chard, and simmer until the spuds are cooked.

Other vegetable recipes

Cauliflower with a garlic and vinegar sauce

coliflor en salsa ajada
This was first eaten in medieval times by vegetarian monks, and it's a good way to jazz up the humble cauliflower. Make sure you choose an ultra-fresh creamy crisp cauli, with no dingy brown patches.

1kg cauliflower
4 cloves of garlic, sliced
75ml olive oil
2 tsp paprika
pinch of cayenne (optional)
2 tbsp sherry vinegar
1 tbsp chopped parsley

Break the cauliflower into large florets and steam, or boil in a small amount of salted water, until just tender. While this is cooking, make the salsa: heat the oil in a small pan over a medium heat and fry the garlic until golden but not brown or burnt. Add the paprika and cayenne and sauté for another minute. Add the sherry vinegar, give it a good stir and pour it over the drained cauliflower. Scatter the parsley over, and serve immediately.

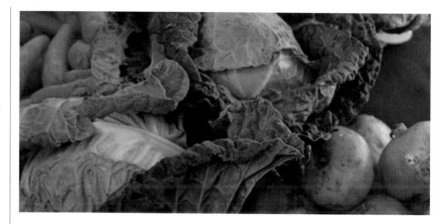

Potatoes with a green sauce

patatas en salsa verde
This is another monastic recipe, thought to help protect against the peste negra, or Black Death.

50ml olive oil
1kg potatoes, peeled, and sliced into 1cm rounds
2 cloves of garlic
4-5 saffron threads
1/2 tsp salt
1 tbsp white wine
4 tbsp chopped parsley
100ml water
2 eggs, beaten

Heat the oil in a large heavy frying-pan over a moderate heat and add the potatoes. Sauté for 15 to 20 minutes, turning the slices occasionally, until they are a light golden brown on both sides. Crush the garlic cloves with the saffron and salt, add the wine to slacken the paste and add this to the pan along with the parsley and water. Give everything a gentle stir, cover the frying-pan with a lid, and leave to cook for another 5 minutes. Stir in the eggs, let them cook through, and serve immediately.

Poor man's potatoes

patatas a lo pobre
This is a peasant dish, and it's completely delicious. It goes especially well with chorizo and eggs: in other words, it's a Spanish cooked breakfast that is eaten at any time of day.

2 green peppers, sliced
50ml olive oil
1kg yellow waxy potatoes
salt and pepper to taste

Fry the green peppers in the oil over a gentle heat until brown at the edges and soft. Slice the potatoes about half a centimetre thick. Mix the slices with the peppers, making sure they're all coated in oil, and season. Cover with a close-fitting lid so that in effect you are steaming as well as frying the ingredients. Stir occasionally and sauté until the potato is properly cooked.

Spinach Jaén-style

espinacas a la jiennense
As the name suggests, this is a favourite tapa
or supper dish in Jaén province.

1kg fresh spinach
50ml olive oil
100g bread
2 cloves of garlic
white pepper and salt
¹/₂ tsp paprika
10ml sherry vinegar
8 quails eggs

Wash the spinach well, and cook in a very
small amount of water. Drain, keeping the
water. Squeeze out any excess water from
the spinach; chop thoroughly. Fry the bread
and garlic and then pound together with the
pepper and paprika. Return the paste to the
pan, adding the spinach, the saved spinach
water and the vinegar. Cook for a few more
minutes. Pile the spinach into a cazuela
(earthenware dish), crack the eggs over
the top, and pop the dish under a hot grill
for a minute until the eggs are cooked.
Serve immediately.

variation
Omit the eggs, and add a tin of chickpeas,
plus a teaspoon of cumin.

Úbeda

Vegetable stew

pisto

This is one of those recipes with infinite variations: tomatoes or squash may also be added, and some people cook everything together, making it indistinguishable from ratatouille. Serve it as a starter, or with fish, or even with a fried egg on top.

3 large red peppers, diced
250g courgettes, sliced
400g aubergines, diced
2 onions, chopped
olive oil, as needed
salt and pepper

The vegetables can be chopped up to the size you fancy – as long as they are all roughly the same size. Sauté each batch of vegetables until soft, but not soggy. Season to taste, and then mix them all together just before serving.

Monastic vegetable stew

alboronia

I am told that this version of a pisto was a speciality of the monasteries in Granada. The quantities given here will serve 5 or 6 people.

50ml olive oil
250g onions, chopped
2 cloves of garlic, crushed
500g potatoes, peeled and quartered
250g fresh tomatoes, chopped
250g green beans
250g butternut squash, cubed
250g green cabbage, sliced
1 tbsp smoked sweet paprika
salt to taste
water

Heat the oil in a casserole dish, add the onions and garlic, and sauté until soft and translucent. Add the rest of the veg and the paprika, season to taste, and give everything a good stir. Fry for another couple of minutes, and then add enough water to submerge the vegetables. Cover the casserole with its lid and leave to simmer gently until everything is cooked.

Meat dishes

Bull's tail stew

rabo de toro

Of course, you're more likely to buy oxtail rather than bull's tail. But that won't make much difference to the overall flavour of the dish, which is typical of Córdoba province.

800g oxtail, cut into portions
2 onions, finely sliced
2 tomatoes, chopped
2 carrots, sliced
50ml olive oil
100ml brandy
100ml red wine
200ml water
1 tbsp sherry vinegar
1 sprig of thyme
1 bayleaf
salt and pepper to taste

Soften the onion in the oil, followed by the carrots and tomatoes. In another pan, brown the meat, flambé the pieces with the brandy and then add the onion mixture followed by the rest of the ingredients. Simmer very, very gently for as long as possible: three hours isn't too long. Take the meat out and blend the sauce. Return the oxtail to the now smooth sauce. The Spanish eat this on its own.

Tripe and chickpea stew

callos a la andaluza
Tripe is a popular tapa and lunchtime dish.
This recipe comes from the advanced
cooking programme at the Escuela de
Hostelería near Baeza. I've omitted the cow's
and pig's feet that were also in the original
version, because the gelatinous nature of
cooking hooves with tripe is too much for all
but the most committed of carnivores.

1kg tripe, already cleaned, cut up into small
pieces
300g chickpeas, soaked
250g morcilla
200g chorizo
1 onion, sliced
50ml olive oil
2 cloves of garlic
1 ham bone
1 tbsp tomato frito (or passata)
$^1/_4$ tsp cloves
$^1/_2$ tsp each of cinnamon and paprika
1 tsp black peppercorns
1 dried chilli

Boil the tripe and chickpeas for 45 minutes.
Fry the onion, garlic, bayleaf and tomato in
the oil until everything is soft and mushy. Add
this to the tripe pot, mix in the spices, along
with the morcilla and chorizo, and continue
cooking until the morcilla has disintegrated
and the chickpeas are tender. Season to taste.

Stewed lamb with almonds

cordero con almendras
This recipe comes from the Granada region,
although over in Cádiz you'll find a very
similar recipe that omits the almonds
but includes carrots, green pepper, thyme
and oregano.

1 onion, sliced
5 cloves of garlic, finely chopped
3 tbsp olive oil
1kg boned shoulder of lamb
5 black peppercorns
$^1/_2$ tsp salt
2 large tomatoes, skinned and chopped
150ml brandy
100g peeled almonds
1 bayleaf
4 saffron threads
water

Fry the onion and garlic in the oil on a low-
to-medium heat until they begin to soften.
Add the lamb, salt and peppercorns to the
pan and sauté on a medium heat, turning
occasionally until the lamb is brown. Add the
tomatoes and fry gently until the tomato
softens a little. Meanwhile chop the almonds,
and then add these, along with the brandy,
bayleaf and saffron, to the meat. Add just
enough water to cover, then put a lid on the
pan and allow to stew gently on top of the
cooker for about 40 minutes.

Moorish kebab

pincho moruno
Pincho moruno or pinchito moruno (little
Moorish kebab) is a very popular Andalucian
fiesta snack, which also makes frequent
appearances in the region's bars as a tapa.
For a classic pinchito moruno you should
really use pork or lamb, but the recipe works
equally well with chicken. Recipes vary quite
a lot, but rather than worrying about the
best combination of spices and seasonings,
the most important thing is to marinade
the meat for several hours in plenty of
garlic and some lemon juice or dry white
wine, along with a generous amount of
cumin and paprika – or whatever spices
you have to hand.

500g pork
1 tbsp olive oil
juice of half a lemon
3 cloves of garlic, crushed
2 tsp ground cumin
2 tsp paprika
1 tsp ground coriander
$^1/_2$ tsp chilli (or to taste)
$^1/_2$ tsp turmeric
pinch of oregano
pinch of salt

Cut the meat into smallish cubes. Mix all the
remaining ingredients together in a bowl.
Stir the meat well into the marinade mixture,
making sure the pieces are all thoroughly
coated. Leave in the fridge for as long as
possible: six hours is good, overnight is better.
When you're ready to cook the kebabs,
remove the meat cubes from the marinade
and thread them onto bamboo skewers
(soaked in water first) and then place them
under the grill, or on a griddle over a medium
heat, until browned and cooked through.

Roast lamb with honey and almonds

cordero asado con miel y almendras
This roast lamb dish is a speciality of the restaurant of the Pedro Antonio de Alarcón cave hotel just outside Guadix in Granada.

1½ kg leg of lamb
2 tbsp runny honey
100ml olive oil
pinch of salt
1 onion, sliced
2 tomatoes, quartered
50g peeled almonds
50g raisins
250ml dry white or rosé wine

Pre-heat the to oven 220°C, gas mark 7. Rinse the lamb and pat dry with kitchen paper. Place in a roasting tray and pour the honey over, followed by the olive oil, and then sprinkle with salt. Strew the onion and tomatoes into the roasting tray around the lamb. Sprinkle the almonds and raisins over everything. Roast for 20 minutes in the hot oven, then pour the wine over the meat and reduce the temperature to 150-170°, gas mark 3, and roast another hour or longer, depending on how well-done you want the lamb to be. Baste occasionally, and keep the bottom of the roasting tray from drying out by adding a little water from time to time.

Danish peace treaty roast lamb

cordero asado
One of several small towns where you can eat this style of roast lamb is Huéscar, where the inhabitants declared war on Denmark in 1809 and only signed a peace treaty in 1981. The Danish and Huéscar's townsfolk are now the greatest of friends and regularly celebrate their peace in the town with this local version of roast segureño lamb.

1kg lamb chops and cutlets
100ml olive oil
½ tsp salt, or to taste
10 medium-sized potatoes, peeled and halved
2 tomatoes, quartered
5 cloves of garlic, whole and unpeeled
1 onion, quartered
2 bayleaves
1 sprig of thyme
300ml white wine
water

Pre-heat the oven to 200°C, gas mark 6. Place the lamb pieces in a roasting tray and pour on the olive oil, then sprinkle with salt. Surround the lamb with the potatoes, tomatoes, garlic, onion, and herbs. Roast for 15 minutes, then pour the white wine into the roasting tray and reduce the temperature to 160°C, gas mark 3, and cook for another hour. Baste the lamb occasionally, and prevent the tray from drying out by adding a little water from time to time.

Braised chorizo in wine

chorizo al vino
This is quirky little recipe that is, in fact, a classic tapa. Some red wines can result in alarmingly purple chorizo; if the vivid hue is too off-putting, either dim the lights or use white wine.

300g chorizo
300ml red (or white) wine

Prick the chorizos with a fork and add them, along with the wine, to a casserole dish. Simmer on a low-to-medium heat for 20 minutes or so until cooked. Serve sliced with hunks of bread.

Meatballs

albóndigas

Meatballs are usually made with a mix of ground pork and beef, probably because the latter was too expensive to use on its own. Best-quality sausages, skins removed, are a handy source of ground pork. In Spain, the sauce served with meatballs is either a rich tomato one, or almond-based. This recipe is inspired by one I came across in a very good cookery book called The Spanish Kitchen, by Nicholas Butcher, now sadly out of print.

for the meatballs:
300g ground beef
200g ground pork
50g breadcrumbs
1 clove of garlic, crushed with a little salt
1 egg, beaten
1 tbsp fresh thyme
3 tbsp chopped parsley
freshly ground black pepper to taste

for the sauce:
50ml olive oil, or 60g lard
1 onion, finely chopped
1 clove of garlic, crushed
4 cherry tomatoes, chopped (or one large flavoursome one)
1 scant tbsp flour
100ml Spanish brandy
100ml fino sherry
1 litre of hot chicken stock, approx
1 bayleaf
50g ground almonds

Mix the meatball ingredients together thoroughly – I usually whiz them all in the food processor, which results in a more finely-textured meatball. Check the seasoning by frying a teaspoon of the mixture. Wet your hands and roll the mixture into walnut-sized balls. Pop them all on an oiled baking tray and bake them in a pre-heated oven at 220°C, gas mark 7, for 20 minutes to brown them. While they are cooking, heat the oil or lard in a casserole dish and sauté the onion and garlic until soft; then add the tomatoes and fry for a few more minutes. Stir in the flour and cook for one minute more, before adding the brandy and sherry. Keep stirring all the while to make a thick sauce, and then pour in the stock – there should be enough liquid to cover the meatballs, which you add now, along with the bayleaf. Leave everything to simmer gently for 15-20 minutes, uncovered. Five minutes before the end of cooking, stir in the ground almonds. These meatballs are great served with mashed potato, but Andalucians, of course, prefer bread.

Pork in olive oil

lomo de orza

This is a classic recipe from Jaén which is a good way of preserving pork meat. The orza refers to the deep earthenware pot that the meat is preserved in.

1kg loin of pork
1 head of garlic
25g cloves
25g black peppercorns
1 litre of olive oil
salt and ground black pepper
2 sprigs of marjoram or oregano
1 orange peel

Slice the meat into 5cm rounds. With the tip of a knife, make small incisions into the meat, large enough to insert a garlic clove, one clove and a peppercorn. Place the meat on a flat dish in one layer, drizzle over a little bit of oil, sprinkle on the marjoram, season with salt and pepper and leave in the fridge overnight.

Next day, fry the meat in some more of the oil over a lively heat, and, once it has browned, reduce the temperature and cook for 20 minutes, turning from time to time. Allow to cool in the pan.

Put everything into sterilized preserving jar, add the orange peel and another marjoram sprig, cover everything with oil and seal. Keep the pork for a couple of weeks before eating it. Apparently, this dish will keep until the next matanza, or pig slaughter, but I have never dared to put this advice to the test.

Chicken with mint and orange juice

pollo con hierbabuena y naranja
There are very few chicken recipes out here – partly, I suspect, because traditionally the animals have been more important as egg-producers and only end up in the pot when their egg-laying days are over. This recipe is also a good way of using up a glut of oranges. And even if you don't happen to have your own citrus orchard, it's still a great dish.

4 chicken breasts
salt, pepper, and oil
150ml freshly squeezed orange juice
2 tbsp chopped fresh mint

Season the breasts with the salt and pepper. Fry them in the oil until they have browned on all sides. Add the orange juice and simmer for 10-15 minutes until the chicken is cooked. Add the mint, and serve.

Mercedes' granny's chicken recipe

pollo al estilo del la abuela alpujarreña
This recipe was given to me by Mercedes Llamas del Castillo, a doctor from Granada. It's a dish her late grandmother, Purificación Vigiana, used to make at home in the Alpujarreño village of Pampaneira. As Mercedes points out, it is very simple to make and a good dish for when you need to rustle up something quick and easy for supper. If you are in a hurry, use chicken breast instead of chicken on the bone. And if you haven't got dried red peppers, add a teaspoonful of mild non-smoked paprika instead. Like the majority of Spanish casserole dishes, this one is not cooked in the oven but on the hob.

1 chicken, cut up into 8 pieces or quartered
50ml olive oil
7 cloves of garlic
3 bayleaves
a few black peppercorns
2 dried red peppers (see page 53)
1 small envelope of Spanish yellow food colouring (optional)
350ml dry white wine
pinch of salt

Peel and slice three of the garlic cloves. Heat the oil in a frying-pan and add the garlic and the chicken. Fry gently until the chicken is brown and nearly cooked through (you may have to do this in batches). Transfer the chicken to a casserole. Rinse and de-seed the peppers, and add them to the casserole, along with the bayleaves, peppercorns, salt and the four remaining whole unpeeled garlic cloves. Pour over the white wine and cook on a low heat for about 20 minutes. If the casserole starts to dry out, add a little water to it.

Stewed partridge

perdiz guisado
The traditional happy ending for children's stories in Spain is "*y comieron perdices y fueron felices*" – and they ate partridge and lived happily ever after.

2-4 partridges
1 onion
1 tomato
1 carrot
1 leek
4 cloves of garlic
3 tbsp olive oil
300ml dry white wine
1 bayleaf
a few black peppercorns
1 sprig of thyme
2 cloves
pinch of saffron
pinch of salt

Chop all the vegetables quite finely and soften them in olive oil for about 10 minutes in a large metal casserole or a very large deep frying-pan. Add the partridge to the vegetables and brown them (add a little more oil if necessary) on a medium heat. As you are frying the partridge you can add the herbs and spices and salt. Remove the partridge, bayleaf and thyme sprig from the pan. Blend the vegetables with a hand-blender until puréed (add a little of the white wine if this helps the process). Return the partridge, bayleaf and thyme to the pan and pour on the puréed vegetables. Add the white wine and gently stew until the partridge is cooked. If the sauce seems a little thick, add some water.

Córdoba

Rabbit stew

conejo guisado

If you don't have dried red peppers,
substitute a red bell pepper and about a
dessertspoon of paprika.

1½ kg rabbit pieces
2 dried red peppers
4 cloves of garlic
1 slice of bread
olive oil
a handful of peeled almonds
200ml dry white wine
pinch of saffron
½ tsp oregano
2 bayleaves
1 sprig of thyme
pinch of salt

Lightly brown the almonds over a medium
heat in a couple of tablespoons of olive oil.
Peel and finely chop the garlic. Add it, along
with the slice of bread, to the frying-pan and
fry on a low heat until the bread is golden.
Remove from the pan. Rinse, peel and core
the peppers and gently soften them on a low
heat in a little more olive oil. Remove from
the pan. In more olive oil, brown the rabbit
pieces (in batches, or adding the pieces
gradually) and add the herbs and salt. Blend
the bread, garlic, almonds and peppers with
a hand blender (adding a little water to the
mixture if necessary) until you have a
smooth paste, or *majado*. Add this to the
rabbit, along with the white wine, and add a
little water if this sauce seems a bit thick.
Cook slowly until the rabbit is done. The
sauce will appear rather orange in colour at
first, but later turns a reddish brown.

Venison in red wine

venado al vino tinto

This is a popular way of dealing with the fruits of a day's hunting in the sierras. Or the supermarket, depending on your inclination.

1 kg venison
1 large onion
6 cloves of garlic
1 small bunch flat-leaf parsley, chopped
½ tsp salt
2 bayleaves
4-5 black peppercorns
1 tsp oregano
2 cloves
pinch of nutmeg
300ml red wine
100ml extra virgin olive oil
500g tomatoes, peeled and chopped

Cut the venison into small pieces and chop up the onion and garlic. Mix all the ingredients together, except the olive oil and the tomato, and leave to marinade overnight. Next day, drain the marinade and put to one side. Heat the olive oil in a pan and add all the ingredients, along with the tomatoes. Sauté everything for 5 minutes, and then add the reserved marinade and allow to reduce for 5 minutes. Add sufficient water to cover the meat, and simmer for an hour. Remove the pieces of meat, and sieve or handblend the cooking liquid to turn it smooth. Return the meat to this sauce, and serve.

Fish dishes

Algeciras fish stew

abaja a la algecireña

Algeciras is the largest port for container ships in the Mediterranean, and this is one of the most interesting local dishes – similar to the bouillabaisse cooked in France.

1½ kg assorted firm-fleshed fish (monkfish, hake, grouper, tuna)
125ml white wine
1 large onion, diced
2 large ripe tomatoes
200ml olive oil
150g fried bread
6 cloves of garlic
a few saffron threads
4 black peppercorns
1 tbsp chopped flat-leaf parsley
salt

Clean the fish, cut into pieces, put into a large saucepan, and add enough water to cover the fish by a couple of centimetres. Add the salt and wine. Bring to the boil, lower the heat, and continue cooking for 15 minutes. Remove the fish from the stock and put to one side.

Take another saucepan or casserole dish and heat half the oil, before adding the onion and one crushed clove of garlic. Sauté until the onion starts to turn golden. Now add the chopped tomato and parsley and continue to cook. After a few minutes, add a third of the stock from the fish. Bring this to the boil and add the bread in small pieces. Add salt to taste, and leave to simmer.

Mash the saffron, black pepper and another clove of garlic with a pestle and mortar. Dilute this paste with two tablespoons or so of the fish stock, add to the soup and continue to simmer for five minutes. The soup by this stage should be quite thick.

Slice, then fry, the remaining garlic cloves in olive oil; add the fish, half cover it with stock, and simmer for a few minutes.

Serve the soup and the fish in separate dishes.

Pepe Gómez' fish sauté

pescado y gambas en salsa de oloroso seco
Pepe lives in El Puerto de Santa María, so it's no surprise that he is quite specific about the kind of sherry to put into this dish: an Osborne oloroso.

2 onions, thinly sliced
3 cloves of garlic, crushed
50ml olive oil
300g shelled raw prawns
4 white fish cutlets (eg hake)
50ml Bailén dry Oloroso
1 small bunch of parsley, chopped
water
salt and pepper

First, make a sofrito: fry the garlic and onion together in a frying-pan with olive oil over a low heat until the onion is soft and mushy, but not brown. Then add the fish, prawns, sherry and parsley and enough water to make a sauce. Season to taste, then simmer until the fish is cooked. If the cutlets are quite thick, they'll need longer cooking than the prawns, so add the latter about 2 or 3 minutes before serving.

Rota-style sea bream

urta a la roteña
As the name says, this recipe comes from Rota on the Huelva coastline. The fish to try and get hold of for this recipe is an urta or blue-spotted sea bream, although any of the bream family would make an acceptable substitute.

1kg sea bream
250ml olive oil
1 large onion, thinly sliced
2-3 large tomatoes, in 1cm slices
1 green pepper, de-seeded and cut into 2cm squares
1 red pepper, de-seeded and cut into 2cm squares
3 cloves of garlic, very finely sliced
1 lemon, sliced
1 bayleaf
8-10 whole black peppercorns

Have your fishmonger gut, clean and scale the fish. Choose an oven dish or tin that is big enough to provide a snug fit for both the fish and veggies. First pour in half the olive oil, then add two-thirds of the chopped peppers, tomatoes, garlic and onion. Tuck a bayleaf into this mixture and season to taste.

Make several deep cuts, to the bone, on both sides of the fish and insert as many lemon slices as will fit into the incisions. Place the fish on top of the vegetables and then add the remaining pieces. Sprinkle the black peppercorns over everything, season lightly with more salt and add the rest of the olive oil. Cook in a pre-heated oven at 180°C, gas mark 4, for 20 minutes.

Dogfish in saffron sauce

cazón en amarillo
This recipe is typical of Cádiz where dogfish is the fish of choice, but it would also work with cod or hake fillets.

1kg potatoes, peeled and halved
4 or 5 saffron threads
1 onion, sliced
3 cloves of garlic, crushed
1 tbsp parsley, chopped
1 green pepper, de-seeded and sliced
50ml olive oil
2 tomatoes
1 slice of fried bread
1/2 tsp salt
75ml fino sherry
1 tsp cumin seeds
1kg dogfish, filleted

Boil the potatoes in enough water to cover them, together with the saffron and bayleaves, until just cooked: this will turn the spuds a sunshine yellow. Do not drain. Meanwhile, sauté the onions and garlic in the olive oil until soft, and then add the green pepper, tomato and parsley and continue frying for another 3 or 4 minutes. Mash the fried bread, salt and cumin in a pestle and mortar, slowly pouring in the fino to make sauce. Put this and the fried vegetables into a blender and blitz until smooth. Then add this liquid to the potatoes, along with the fish. Simmer until the fish is cooked – how long will depend on the thickness of the steaks – and serve hot.

Marinaded sardines

sardinas en adobo

This marinade is also good with anchovies or mackerel. For more robust fish, the marinade would include vinegar rather than wine and the fish would be deep-fried, not grilled as is the case here. Just to confuse things, around Cádiz, the vinegar and deep-fry method is called *bienmesabe* (literally, it tastes good to me) – which is also the name of an angel's-hair pumpkin jam pudding from Málaga.

5 cloves of garlic
1 tsp each of oregano, peppercorns, cumin
   seeds, and salt
100ml olive oil
100ml white wine
1kg sardines, cleaned
4 tbsp flour

Use a pestle and mortar to make a paste with the garlic, oregano, peppercorns, salt and cumin. Then whisk the oil, wine and garlic paste together to make a marinade. Cover the fish with the marinade and leave for 6 hours. Strain off the liquid, dip the sardines in flour (a good way to do this is to gently shake the fish and flour together in a plastic bag), and then shallow fry them in a little more oil until cooked and crispy – how long will depend on how big the sardines are.

Desserts

The Andalucians don't enthuse about desserts in the same way the Italians or the French do. Of course there are lots of well-known recipes, but the quintessentially Spanish sweets such as rice pudding, *arroz con leche*, or creme caramel, *flan*, have their origins in the northern milk-producing areas. Down in Andalucía, people may nibble sweet biscuits and pastries at any opportunity during the day, but you'll find that fresh fruit is the most common way of finishing a meal.

Olive oil ice cream

helado de aceite de oliva

It may sound a bit of an unlikely combination, but actually the grassy peppery taste of olive oil makes it a wonderful ice cream to serve with soft fruit such as raspberries or peaches. The recipe was given to me by the chefs' training school in Baeza, and the key to success is definitely to use only the freshest and the very best ingredients you can lay your hands on – especially the olive oil. Ice cream tasting like axle grease seldom wins plaudits.

1 litre of full-fat milk
250g caster sugar
8 egg yolks
200g extra virgin olive oil

Pour the milk into a large heavy-bottomed saucepan, place it over a low heat and bring it slowly to just below boiling point. Meanwhile, put the egg yolks and sugar into a bowl and beat hard with an electric whisk until the mixture thickens and doubles in volume. Still beating continuously, add the oil little by little until it is all mixed in. As the milk starts to steam – but before it bubbles – remove it from the heat and pour it slowly into the mixture, continuing to whisk as you do so. Leave to cool before decanting into an ice cream maker, following the manufacturer's instructions. If you don't have an ice cream maker, just use a lidded container and put the custard into the freezer. Remember to stir the mixture at intervals with a fork, to break up the ice crystals.

Serves six.

Sherry ice cream

helado de oloroso

This is another custard-based ice cream, but this time sweet sherry is added instead of the olive oil. You could use a Pedro Ximénez, but my preference is for a sweet oloroso. And my favourite way of serving it is to squidge the freshly churned frozen cream between two slices of just warm, crunchy on the outside, but sticky in the middle, chocolate brownies.

500ml double cream
250ml full-fat milk
1 vanilla pod
8 egg yolks
100g caster sugar
100ml sweet sherry

Put the cream and milk into a saucepan. Split the vanilla pod lengthways and scrape the sticky innards over the milk and slowly bring it to just below boiling point.

Beat the sugar and egg yolks with an electric whisk until pale, and then whisk in the milk. Return this to the pan and heat gently until the custard thickens enough to coat the back of a spoon. Stir frequently, and don't feel tempted to hasten the process by turning up the heat – you'll end up with scrambled custard. Chill both the custard and the sherry in the fridge for a couple of hours, then churn the custard in your ice cream maker until it's nearly frozen before adding the sherry. Alcohol has a lower freezing point and it can take ages for the ice cream to turn solid if sherry is added at the beginning. Serves six.

variation
Soak 100g of Málaga raisins in the sherry and include these when you add it.

Heavenly bacon

tocino de cielo

You've got to eat to put on weight, slim women are admonished. Well, this pudding will certainly help you do that. Commonly called heavenly bacon, this is a cinnamon flavoured creme caramel.

225g sugar
8 egg yolks, beaten
1 lemon rind, grated
cinnamon
250ml water

Put the water, sugar, lemon rind and cinnamon stick into a heavy saucepan and bring to the boil. Make a thick syrup that passes the thread test: when dropped from a spoon, it forms a syrupy thread. Leave to cool a little, and then, beating all the time, pour it into the egg yolks. Strain this mixture and then ladle it into little square moulds or ramekins, at the bottom of which you've caramelised some sugar. To do this, just blast a sprinkling of sugar with your blowtorch until it's pale caramel in colour.

Put the ramekins into a bain marie and simmer in a moderate oven until cooked. As with a cake, when a skewer comes out clean, the custard is cooked. Leave to cool.

Custard cream pots

natillas

This is based on a recipe from López Correa, a restaurant in Granada, where they do some very good home cooking.

1 litre of whole milk
4 egg yolks
4 tbsp sugar
lemon peel
2 tsp cornflour
4 plain biscuits or ginger biscuits

Boil the milk with half the sugar and the lemon peel. Beat the yolks with the rest of the sugar and the cornflour. Take the milk off the heat and beat gradually into the cornflour, avoiding lumpiness. Return to a very gentle heat, and stir with a wooden spoon until thick. The mixture mustn't boil.

Put some biscuit into the bottom of a ramekin and pour in the custard. Dust with cinnamon, and chill in the fridge until needed.

Rice pudding

arroz con leche

The only fond memory I have of school food is rice pudding; it was about the only instance of a spice being used in generally mean-minded kitchens, and I was particularly partial to the thick nutmeggy milk-skin that formed over the rice. The Spanish version is much more elegant and just as delicious. It is made by simmering the rice, not the British way of baking it.

1 litre of milk
100ml single cream
2cm piece of orange peel
3cm stick of cinnamon
150g short-grain rice
200g caster sugar
ground cinnamon to serve

Bring the milk, cream, orange peel and cinnamon stick to the boil in a large heavy-bottomed saucepan. Just as it starts to bubble, add the rice and keep stirring until everything comes back to the boil. Add the sugar and simmer gently until the rice is tender and the milk has been absorbed. Remove the orange peel and cinnamon stick and divide the pudding between small bowls – it looks more appetizing in small quantities – and leave to cool in the fridge. Before serving dust each bowl with a little ground cinnamon.

variation

Use a vanilla pod and omit the cinnamon stick.

Books, contacts and websites

Further information

If this book has inspired you to find out more about food and wine in Andalucía, here are some suggestions that may help you.

Books

A selection of cookery books that we've admired and liked:

The charming *The Flavours of Andalucía* by Elizabeth Luard (Collins and Brown, 1991), is also illustrated by her. More recently she has written *The Food of Spain and Portugal* which contains a section on the region.

Sam and Sam Clark's *Casa Moro* (Ebury Press) is an account of their culinary experiences and family life in the Alpujarras. Being star chefs, their recipes aren't confined to the region, but it's a very evocative book.

Anyone interested in sherry should have a copy of Julian Jeffs' *Sherry* (Mitchell Beazley) – he knows absolutely everything and everyone in the business, and this entertaining book is essential reading.

Spanish speakers could also search out:

Gazpachos, Sopas y Ajos Blancos by Enrique Mapelli López (Editorial Arguval), which collates every variation of gazpacho under the sun.

Cocina Casera Andaluza by Ángel López Elvira (Editorial Arguval) has an excellent selection of no-nonsense recipes.

El Valle de la Alegría by L. Benavides-Barajas (Editorial Dulcinea) is a quirky little book on this valley in Granada province. It contains a bit of history, and has plenty of recipes and information about local and traditional Andalucian foods and ingredients.

Spanish foodstuffs in the UK

Spanish food and wine is fairly easy to find – the Brindisa brand is particularly worth looking out for, retailing through supermarkets and delis. Lucky Londoners can head for their direct outlets at Exmouth Market in Clerkenwell, and Borough Market under London Bridge; check out their website at www.brindisa.com for further details. Also worth checking out is La Alacena (UK) Ltd. Tel: 01604 784 159, www.alacena.co.uk.

Websites

For general information, try the Andalucian tourist board www.andalucia.org, and also www.andalucia.com, which covers everything from holidays to living in the region. The provinces each have a website too, and the best of these is www.turismosevilla.org.

Sherry lovers might also like to take a look at www.tenstartapas.com

For more information on alternative and organic lifestyles, La Chispa magazine has a website: www.lachispa.net.

Roger Davies runs tailored gourmet tours and cookery classes. www.aqot.com.

Further information on Carmen Ladrón's contemporary arts centre and hotel La Cartuja de Cazalla de la Sierra is at www.skill.es/cartuja

And lastly, of course, if you have any comments or suggestions about this book, then do let us know via our website: www.thetasteofaplace.com. We'd love to hear from you.

Acknowledgments

Huge thanks to everyone who made our research in Andalucía such fun:

Juan Carlos Alonso; Pablo Amate; Edward Butler, Grupo Estévez; Martín Coranado, Hotel Escuela La Laguna; José Gómez, Osborne group; Victoria González-Gordon, González-Byass; Alexander Koch, Ines Rosales; Carmen Ladrón de Guevara Bracho; Ignacio López de Carrizosa Domecq, Bodegas Tradición; Elisabeth Luard; Willy Moya, owner chef of La Cartuja and Poncio restaurants; Jan Pettersen, Fernando de Castilla; Ruth Roberts; The Sherry Institute in London; Julian Sanjuan, Museo del Vino Málaga; Mercedes Santamaría Vázquez and Pilar Pla, El Sierra Maestro; María José Sevilla, Foods from Spain; María Carmen Cardona Rojas and her daughter Carolina; James Carter; Steven Donegan; Ricardo Del Cid; Eladio Ferrer; Cristina Flores; Don Rafael de la Fuente; Paca García Sierra; Francisco Lillo; Mercedes Llamas del Castillo; Jesús López; Antonio López de la Casa; Juan Carlos Muñoz Casares; Sir Frank Price; M & H Price, butchers and fishmongers of Harborne High Street, Birmingham; La Porrona; Agustín Rodríguez; Francisco Titos; Fuensanta Martín Cáceres; Antonio Gallardo.

Many thanks also to our long-suffering editor Jonathan Wetton, who wrestled again with our grammar, spellings and styles, and made sense of what we'd written.

Finally, thanks to our families for being such willing guinea pigs when it came to testing the recipes.

Photography © Chakula Press Ltd except:
© Héloïse McGuinness pages 1, 2, 4 (col 3), 10, 13, 14, 15, 16, 17, 25 (col 1), 34, 35, 36, 38, 53, 54, 68, 77, 81, 84 (col 1), 105, 108, 111, 113, 118, 120 (col 2), 127, (col 2).
© Osborne Group page 62
© Manolo Manosalbas pages 18, 19, 124

Index